A Spiritual Journey to Unwavering Faith: A Multi-Denominational, Multi-Dimensional Spiritual Journey

Published by Gatekeeper Press
2167 Stringtown Rd, Suite 109
Columbus, OH 43123-2989
www.GatekeeperPress.com

The content and editorial work of this book are entirely the product of the author. Leonel Montes de Oca of Eyecandy Studios created and designed the cover and all illustrations. Gatekeeper Press did not participate in and is not responsible for any aspect of these elements.

ISBN (hardcover): 9781662930416
ISBN (paperback): 9781662930423
eISBN: 9781662930430

A SPIRITUAL JOURNEY TO UNWAVERING FAITH

A MULTI-DENOMINATIONAL, MULTI-DIMENSIONAL SPIRITUAL JOURNEY

DAVE SCELBA
Author

LEO MONTES DE OCA
Illustrator

gatekeeper press™

Columbus, Ohio

I dedicate this book to the most precious and important people in my life. My wife Jody, son Kris, daughter Jessie, daughter-in-law Sue, son-in-law Mike, six grandchildren: Nicky; Joey; Sofia; Gia; Sienna; Mikey; and my extended family of very best friends.

God has truly blessed me.

Chapters   Page

APPENDUM

Chapter 1
Introduction

2 Corinthians 5:7

We live by what we believe, not by what we can see.

Almost everyone at some point in their lives questions their faith and/or belief in God. Even the most learned religious scholars, ordained and lay leaders, and faith-based teachers admit to having doubt at times.

Uncertainty or even disbelief is understandable. We live in a troubling world and are constantly barraged with fear, terror, war, discrimination, and hate.

We can't escape from witnessing people around the world experiencing the horrors of pain, sickness, disease, anguish, and suffering. So, it's only natural for these heartbreaking factors to overshadow God's love for us and to question God's existence. These negative influencers can easily test our faith and instill a strong sense of doubt.

I wrestled with faith and a belief in God for many years, but I feel blessed to have experienced a series of life-changing events that opened my eyes, heart, and mind. I now have no doubt in God's existence, and I have a deep unwavering faith and belief in an afterlife.

Let me give you a brief idea of my background. Both my parents were teachers, and my father was also a professional musician and renowned flutist. So, I became a music teacher with an ambition to become an administrator. When the opportunity to leave teaching for the business world presented itself, I took it. After a few years of being employed in corporate organizations, I became an entrepreneur. Working in the fast-paced competitive marketing industry, I constantly faced financial challenges as well as ongoing physical and mental stress. The daily grind caused me to become a skeptical, judgmental, and jaded person.

I have no formal religious education. I'm not a theologian or biblical scholar and no one would consider me to be a "fire and brimstone" preacher or bible thumper.

Like most people of Italian descent, I was raised as a Roman Catholic and the town I grew up in had a homogeneous population comprised of fifty percent Catholic and fifty percent Jewish families. My wife was the first Protestant I ever met, and I became a Presbyterian (a Protestant Denomination) after my children began attending the First Presbyterian Church, USA.

I became truly involved and served several terms as an ordained Elder helping to manage the church finances, and as a Deacon where I enjoyed providing pastoral services and participating on missions that cared for people within our community.

Deacons take a vow to serve through honoring scripture as the reliable word of God. To be a better informed and knowledgeable ordained Deacon, I began reading and self-studying the bible and scriptures. Helping the diversified members of our community also meant understanding and appreciating its various faiths of Christians, Jews, and Muslims. These three major world religions worship the same God and share much of the Old Testament as the foundation of their faiths.

So why is there so much religious conflict and disagreement throughout the world?

Some may feel there are many reasons, but I think the primary reason for conflicts and disagreements is because of the human interpretations of scripture … and humans are fallible.

Almost all the Old Testament was written in Hebrew with some sections written in Aramaic because this was the native tongue of Jesus and many of his followers. The New Testament was written in Greek and then both Testaments were translated into Greek. From Greek, the Bible was translated into many languages, including Latin, which was the foundation to the Romance languages, before being translated into English as we know it. So, it makes sense to believe many things may have either been lost or mis-interpreted over 2,000 years of translations. Humans were the transcription translators and humans make the interpretations. To further complicate the situation, scripture can have multiple meanings to multiple people. That's the inspirational beauty of scripture, but it's also the reason for many religious conflicts and disagreements.

Interpretation of scripture can easily vary from reader to reader. Even the same reader can find new meanings in passages they previously read depending on their current state of mind and affairs.

There is an old saying that there are times when people need their churches, synagogues or mosques and times when the churches, synagogues and mosques need their people. Organized religion has helped billions of people over the course of time. But it has also historically been at the center of political and financial corruption and at the root of the most vicious religious wars of all time.

Unfortunately, some religious leaders intentionally misuse scripture to gain power and money, and to control a gullible and uneducated population. They use it as a tool of judgement, keeping people of different faiths separated and at odds with one and another ... human fallibility.

Perhaps, a common belief of one God, but too many interpretations of His word.

I wonder, if scripture had the same universal meaning to everyone, would we be living in a happier, loving, and peaceful world?

Over the years of writing this book, I interviewed and spoke with many people of different faiths and beliefs, including agnostics and atheists.

Except for those that professed to be atheists, almost everyone else had some sense or level of spirituality and belief in a higher power. I've been blessed to experience many remarkable events that are beyond any possibility of coincidences.

These experiences converted my doubts into unwavering faith, my skepticisms into a total belief in God and the afterlife, and led me to discover the true power of prayer.

I have no doubt these events were signs and messages delivered to me confirming God's existence and to strengthen my own faith. I also feel God has given me the mission and charter to provide comfort to those in need, and to use my experiences to help anyone who wishes to experience their own personal journey to discovering faith.

My spiritual journey to discovering faith began about a year before my father-in-law, Al Kain, died and became stronger with the passing of my father, Frank, and mother, Irma.

My father-in-law and parents all died in my arms. As they took their last breaths, I asked them to please give me a sign and do whatever they could, if possible, to confirm the existence of God and the afterlife.

Literally moments after they each passed and many times since, they all communicated with me and provided profound signs that were personal connections we had between us. I'm very thankful these signs and communications continue to this day.

Like anyone would, I initially attributed these events to be sheer coincidences. But after experiencing a series of these unique, strange, unexplainable encounters, I realized I was witnessing events that went far beyond the obvious, and in many circumstances could not be identified using my five key senses.

Once I accepted the possibility a higher power may be at work, my eyes, heart, and mind were opened to a whole new world or realm.

During the discovery process of my spiritual journey, I read many books that included historical mythology, afterlife experiences, spiritual enlightenment, faith, the Old and New Testaments of several different Bible translations and versions, excerpts of the Koran, Divine Interventions, and devotionals written by laypersons from around the world.

I especially enjoyed reading devotionals by people of all walks of life who told their stories through essays that connected to specific scripture. Their personal experiences relating to selected scripture were genuine, insightful, and deeply moving.

Devotionals inspired me to research relevant scripture that had a direct correlation to my unique experiences. Linking scriptures to the events I was experiencing and witnessing provided another perspective on what couldn't be defined or identified with my key senses. When I was researching scriptures, I referenced a variety of bibles, including: NRSV (New Revised Standard Version); NIV (New International Version Study Bible); New American, New Century Version, Centennial Bible New Testament and NKJV (New King James Version).

As a result of working through the process, I've come to have compassion, even sympathy for those who can only believe in what they see, hear, taste, touch, or smell. They have a safe, logical thought process based upon proof and data that is provided by solely utilizing their five key senses.

Again, it's just my opinion, but I truly feel they are missing out on many of God's greatest gifts. The world would be a better place if more people had faith that there is living beyond what is seen, and could accept a higher power that provides love and freedom.

During my research, it was interesting to learn how the philosophies and life recommendations quoted in so many modern day spiritual and self-help books and materials are rooted in scripture. Some can be found in the appendix of this book.

As I connected my personal events to specific scriptures, I realized everything I was searching for was already compiled for me in one comprehensive best-selling book … the Bible. While the Bible is often referred to as a book, it's really a canon, an agreed compilation of writings throughout time to try and mark the activity of God and written by many authors inspired by God.

To be honest, the Bible can be confusing, difficult to comprehend and not the easiest book to read. The pages dedicated to dates, geographic locations, and family genealogy can be a bit boring, but they are important points of history of the past, present, and future, and serve as a reliable witness of God's activity and details the lineage of Jesus from David.

Buried within the historical text are wonderful, fascinating stories, prayers and Psalms that literally address every possible human emotion, challenge, or situation.

2 Timothy 3:16–17

All scripture is inspired by God and is useful for teaching, for reproof, for correction, and for training in righteousness, so that everyone who belongs to God may be proficient, equipped for every good work.

Scriptures provide answers to the questions of every human emotion and issues like love; marriage; family; sexuality; hope; faith; peace; success; money; satisfaction; celebration; friendship; fellowship; citizenship; and stewardship. Scriptures also speak to forgiveness; discouragement; worry; concern; loneliness; depression; guilt; confusion; jealousy; envy; fear; anger; temptation; rejection; dysfunction; drinking; substance abuse; troubles; distress; sickness; illness; plagues; pandemics; time management; and so much more.

Jeremiah 31:21

Set-up road markers for yourself, make yourself signposts; consider well the highway, the road by which you went ...

The Bible provides the road map to surrendering your fears over to God ... instruction on conquering the challenges of forgiveness ... teaches how to share your love and accept others love ... controlling the process of judgement and the power of prayer or meditation to discover wisdom, strength, and patience.

The Bible provides the guidance, wisdom, and instruction to finding happiness in a world filled with perpetual turmoil, sickness, tragedies, despair, sadness, jealousy, envy and what every living creature in this world will experience and so many fear … death. Scriptures provide us with hope, new life, happiness, grace, peace, joy, and much needed love.

Joshua 1:8

This book of law shall not depart out of your mouth; you shall meditate on it day and night, so that you may be careful to act in accordance with all that is written in it. For then you shall make your way prosperous, and then you shall be successful.

A Spiritual Journey to Discovering Faith details my unique experiences, and the purpose in sharing my spiritual journey is to give those with doubt, a sense of comfort, peace, and hope. I also wish to provide confirmation and inspiration to those who already have faith, and to hopefully strengthen their existing belief.

Luke 6:40

A student is not better than the teacher, but the student who has been fully trained will be like the teacher.

Only God has the power to change the world and I certainly don't believe I have the power to move mountains, but I can try to be a modern-day disciple. My goal in writing this book and sharing my personal spiritual experiences is to hopefully inspire and enrich one person's life, who will go on to share and inspire another person's life and they go on to touch another and yet another.

2 Timothy 2:2

You should teach people whom you can trust the things you and many others have heard me say. Then they will be able to teach others.

Enlightening numbers of people willing to pay it forward by sharing in God's word and messages would be a wonderful legacy to leave after I'm gone. I pray this book enriches your own spiritual journey and inspires you to share your experiences with others.

Thanks for reading, and may God Bless You!

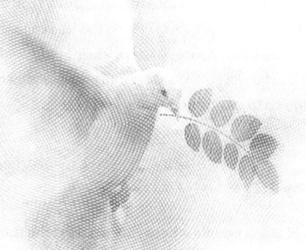

Chapter 2
Inspiration to share

Job 4:20

Between morning and evening, they are destroyed: they perish forever without any regarding it.

I was initially inspired to write this book after the sudden and unexpected death of my beloved father-in-law, Alan Kain. So many strange and unexplainable events occurred just prior to his death and for two years following his passing that I was compelled to document everything that had happened. I also felt I had an obligation, even a moral responsibility, to share my experiences with those who are wrestling with their faith, the belief in God, and who may be looking for comfort or in need of some reassuring words.

Philemon 15:16

Perhaps this is the reason he was separated from you for a while, so that you might have him back forever, no longer as a slave but more than a slave, a beloved brother – especially to me but how much more to you, both in the flesh and in the Lord.

At first, I simply thought these events were just coincidences. But after witnessing a series of unexplainable events, I couldn't ignore the possibility that there was more to what I was experiencing … something beyond a worldly explanation.

The episode that occurred with my father-in-law at the exact moment my second grandson, Joseph, was born in 2010 was amazing and the pivotal point that my life was changed forever.

Daniel 7:1

In the first year of King Bel-shaz'-zar of Babylon, Daniel had a dream and visions in his head as he lay in bed. Then he wrote down the dream.

Time can alter or change one's memory, so I realized it would be important to document and record each of these experiences as they occurred. Even before I began writing this book, I wanted accurate evidence and a detailed record of these events for my own personal future recollections.

Ephesians 1:18-19

So that, with the eyes of your heart enlightened, you may know what is hope to which He has called you, what are the riches of His glorious inheritance among the saints, and what is the immeasurable greatness of His power for us who believe, according to the working of His great power.

For years, I'd start and stop writing and I'd go back once or twice each year, re-read and re-edit. But I was never satisfied or happy with my writing. The details were there, but it lacked an inspirational message and I felt readers deserved better.

So, I filed it away in 2013 and resolved myself to the fact that writing was a therapeutic way for me to accept the loss of my father in-law. At the very least, I had an accurate, historical record of each unexplainable event surrounding his passing. Each of us in our lifetime will experience happy times and sad times. There are no exceptions.

Psalms 145:7

They shall celebrate the fame of Your abundant goodness and shall sing aloud of Your righteousness.

Five months after the death of my father-in-law in 2008 we celebrated the birth of our first grandson, Nicholas, in January 2009 and one year later we welcomed our second grandson, Joseph, in January 2010. We were later blessed with the births of four more healthy grandchildren, Sofia, Giavanna, Sienna, and Michael David, in the following years. In 2019, my wife retired as a public school teacher, and I joined her by executing succession plans for several companies I created.

Psalms 40:1

I waited patiently for the Lord, He turned to me and heard my cry.

Our sad times included personal illness, the deaths of both my parents and a loving uncle and the sudden death of a business partner whom I worked with for over 30 years. An overwhelming amount of stress created from difficult family situations and monumental business and financial challenges, as well.

Then in February of 2020 the world as we knew it drastically changed. Everyone, regardless of where they lived in the world, shared the same Covid-19 pandemic health crisis. No one was immune or protected from this deadly disease and I found it hard not to view this as a possible biblical event designed to cleanse the world or give us all a loud wake up call.

Psalm 15:2

Wash me thoroughly from my inequity, and cleanse me of my sin.

Covid-19 literally affected everyone in every part of the world with no exceptions. All nations and all people faced the same stressful life or death health and financial challenges.

I found it interesting that like faith, the Coronavirus could not be detected with our key senses. The Covid-19 virus couldn't be seen or heard, it had no taste or smell, and it had no feel to the touch. Our key senses couldn't identify its deadly presence.

Hebrews 11:1-3

Now faith is the assurance of things hoped for, the conviction of things not seen. Indeed, by faith our ancestors received approval. By faith we understand that the worlds were prepared by the word of God, so that what is seen was made visible from things that are not visible.

My wife and I had always talked about spending a few months during the winter in Naples, Florida, but we weren't sure we could emotionally handle being away from our children and grandchildren for an extended period of time.

So, as a test we rented a condo in Naples, Florida from our dear friends Sil and Muffy. It was during the first week of our vacation when the crisis struck the United States and New Jersey was a hot spot for the virus. The entire world went into lockdown and while our children and grandchildren were locked down in Northern New Jersey, it was smarter and safer for us to remain in Naples, Florida.

We considered ourselves truly blessed when Sil and Muffy asked us to stay with them at their fabulous resort home in Tiburon, located on the grounds of the Ritz Carlton. It was hard not to feel a bit guilty because we were in a warm, safe, spectacular environment while our family was in a lockdown in New Jersey, one of the country's most infected hot spots.

We were very cautious and adhered to the CDC guidelines and health professional's recommendations and isolated ourselves for nearly three months.

Experiencing a worldwide pandemic gave confirmation that no one is immune from evil, deadly forces.

Faith, that also could not be identified through our key senses of sight, sound, touch, taste, or smell provided those who believe much needed hope, that we'd get through the worst pandemic experience of our lifetime. The Covid-19 crisis inspired me to complete this book.

Chapter 3
The Serenity Prayer

"God, grant me the serenity to accept the things I cannot change, the courage to change the things I can, and the wisdom to know the difference."

My spiritual journey began the day I read an enlightening book titled "Life Lessons" by Elisabeth Kubler-Ross and David Kessler.

I read those 27 powerful words on page 195, in chapter twelve and my life was forever changed.

Being raised Roman Catholic and living in a community that lacked religious diversity, I had never heard of the Serenity Prayer. Discovering the Serenity Prayer made me realize I was a religious, and more importantly, a spiritual neophyte.

Because I believe this prayer truly gets to the essence of life, I feel compelled to provide a brief explanation.

The Serenity Prayer was written by a theologian-philosopher and Protestant Pastor named Reinhold Niebuhr. He used some of the phrases during his sermons and preaching throughout the 1930's and in 1943 he composed and delivered his most famous Sermon, "The Serenity Prayer." His prayer has been edited, plagiarized, and widely republished by all types of support groups, from the US Army to hospital cancer centers, to literally every addiction and 12-step program imaginable and more. The most popular and commonly known edited version consists of only 27 short, profoundly powerful words.

Reinhold Niebuhr's full version of the Prayer is even more prolific.

God, give us grace to accept with serenity the things that cannot be changed, Courage to change the things which should be changed, and the Wisdom to distinguish the one from the other.

Living one day at a time, Enjoying one moment at a time, Accepting hardship as a pathway to peace, Taking, as Jesus did, This sinful world as it is, Not as I would have it, Trusting that You will make all things right, If I surrender to Your will, So that I may be reasonably happy in this life, And supremely happy with You forever in the next.

Amen.

The edited 27-word version is worth repeating and linking to specific scripture:

"God, grant me the serenity to accept the things I cannot change, the courage to change the things I can, and the wisdom to know the difference."

1 Peter 5:7

Give all your worries over to Him, because He cares about you.

-And-

John 14:1

Jesus said "Don't let your hearts be troubled. Trust in God, and trust in me."

It makes no sense to stress out and worry about things you have no control over. It's very difficult, but making yourself sick over something you have absolutely no control over will not change things. Having faith and surrendering your worries and burdens over to God and trusting in Him to carry you through every situation will provide you with peace and resolve.

"God grant me the serenity to accept the things I cannot change, the courage to change the things I can, and the wisdom to know the difference."

Joshua 1:9

I hereby command you: Be strong and courageous; do not be frightened or dismayed, for the Lord your God is with you wherever you go.

Proverbs 3:5-6

Trust the Lord with all you heart, and don't depend on your own understanding. Remember the Lord in all you do, and He will give you success.

If you have faith God has a plan for you, you'll believe every personal and business situation or opportunity is being presented to you by God. He is guiding you down a path where there is no failure. At that moment, you may not think it's a right decision or feel it's the best thing to do, but trust in God because he has a better plan for your future.

There is an old Yiddish proverb that says you can spend all your time planning for the future, and God sits back and laughs.

Believing God is the Holy Spirit, and that the Holy Spirit resides in each of us, helps us to accept God's presence. The Holy Spirit provides us with options, directions, and opportunities. But it's up to each of us to have the courage to make decisions without concern and fear of failure.

"God grant me the serenity to accept the things I cannot change, the courage to change the things I can, and the wisdom to know the difference."

James 1:5

But if any of you needs wisdom, you should ask God for it, He is generous and enjoys giving to all people, so He gives you wisdom.

Book smarts, passing tests or getting good grades may be a sign of intelligence, but they aren't Wisdom. Wisdom is the ability to recognize and accept what is and what isn't in your control. Wisdom is the gift of being able to surrender yourself to God. And Wisdom is the process of making fearless decisions and trusting that God has your back.

Job 11:5-6

But oh, that God would speak. And open His lips to you, and that He would tell you the secret of wisdom! For wisdom is many sided. Know then that God exacts of you less than your guilt deserves.

The first thing I do during my daily prayers is to thank God for everything He does for me, my family, and my friends. But the second thing I ask for everyday is Wisdom, because Wisdom gives me faith.

Chapter 4
Sharing Wisdom

In July of 2020 at the height of the Covid-19 crisis, and when civil unrest was running rampant in our streets, I was asked to deliver a sermon to our congregation.

I felt God was instructing me to re-introduce our congregation to the Serenity Prayer and Psalm 23. As I began to write, His words just poured out of my mind. These two prayers interlaced with key scripture provided the essence of what people were yearning to hear.

Churches were shut down and closed to their members, so my sermon was given via a Zoom Video Production.

After preparing the text, my good friend and long-time creative collaborator, Leo Montes de Oca, used his God-given talents to bring my words to life.

Sermon of July 19th, 2020

We are all experiencing the most unsettling, scary, stressful, and for many, the loneliest times of our lives. The Covid-19 pandemic followed by horrible acts of civil disobedience and social unrest makes me feel like I'm witnessing the prophecy of Revelations. The only thing missing so far are the presence of seven spirits, seven churches, seven golden lampstands, and seven stars. Things are so bleak; I'm just waiting for the seventh angel to blow the seventh trumpet to fulfill the mystery of God.

Obviously, I'm just kidding. But doesn't it seem like we're experiencing catastrophic events of biblical proportions?

And who knows, maybe God is sending the whole world a very loud wake-up call. And there is no escaping the constant barrage of bad news that's just impossible to ignore. The media thrives on publishing and broadcasting society's faults and violence. Media falsely claims to be concerned, yet they aggressively promote the worst of mankind simply to increase ratings. And it's like watching a bad car wreck … you just can't turn away.

Our Lord's teachings of tolerance have been replaced by law breakers' rationalization to disregard and disrespect one and another. And again, the media's continual promotion of this uncivil behavior is all enveloping … and consuming every minute of our daily lives.

People have different views about the authenticity or actual origins of scripture. But it really doesn't matter what your position or opinion may be. Reading scripture can help comfort you and carry you through the most emotionally challenging times of your life. And these are certainly pretty difficult times of crisis.

So, let's address a few key emotions with relative scripture passages.

Worry … this is a tough emotion to control or conquer. Let's face it, you'd have to have a heart of stone not to be deeply concerned about what's happening. But it's very important to differentiate or distinguish concern from worry. As some of you know, I recite the Serenity Prayer literally every day and lately multiple times a day. While this isn't scripture, they are wonderful, brilliant life-changing words written by the theologian - philosopher and Protestant Pastor, Reinhold Niebuhr.

This is the edited version with my interpretation.

"God grant me the serenity to accept the things I cannot change."

To worry about things you have absolutely no control over is foolish and if you think about it, insulting to God. To be totally consumed with worry is putting yourself on the same level as God or thinking you're His equal. It's also admitting you have no faith or trust in God. You adhere to all the Covid-19 protocols of social distancing, wearing a mask and sanitizing your hands every time you wave to someone. But there is a chance you may still contract this dreaded disease. If you put your faith in God first and receive the proper medical attention … believe you will get well and healthy again.

"The courage to change the things you can."

If you truly believe the Holy Spirit is in you, God's hand will guide you and God will give you the courage and strength to do the right things. Our church is filled with people who have had the courage to reach out into our community and connect with those who are less fortunate. There are a lot of people in the world who donate money, but would never consider co-mingling in neighborhoods with those who are less fortunate, purely out of the fear they may put themselves in physical danger. The members of our congregation are fearless, and courageously serve food, provide clothing and most importantly, aren't afraid to share their love with our neighbors in need. It's difficult to witness what's happening in our society today.

But we can hold our heads high and be proud because we have the courage to be true disciples of our Lord and Savior, Jesus Christ.

"And the Wisdom to know the difference."

It took me over 50 years to understand and find the humility to accept that I'm not in control. Wisdom begins with being humble and then doing an honest self-assessment. Being the CEO and President of many companies over the years, people would give me things like "The Boss" coffee mug.

And after years of receiving these ego-building items, you begin to believe you really do have control over everything.

So, it was a very difficult lesson for me to learn, but once I accepted, I'm not the Boss and discovered how to surrender my worries over to God, I finally began to live with hope and found my inner peace.

1 Peter 5:7 and Psalm 91:2 speaks to worries.

1 Peter 5:7

Give all your worries to Him because He cares about you.

-And-

Psalm 91:2

Those who go to God Most High for safety will be protected by the Almighty. I will say to the Lord, "You are my place of safety and protection. You are my God and I trust you."

Fear and stress are two more negative and destructive emotions that seamlessly integrate with worry. In fact, worry leads to fear and fear leads to stress. It's a vicious cycle so many people fall into and it's very difficult to break that cycle once it begins. And it seems this emotional roller coaster is always centered around two primary catalysts … health and wealth. But remember:

Psalm 103:3

He forgives all my sins and heals all my diseases.

-And-

Philippians 4:19

My God will use His wonderful riches in Christ Jesus to give you everything you need.

Reciting the Serenity Prayer can help to bring you peace and hope, but taking the time to embrace scripture that speaks to your current emotions will help to enrich your spiritual journey and provide guidance when you need it most.

2 Timothy 1:7 and Proverbs 3:25-26 speak to fear.

2 Timothy 1:7

God did not give us a spirit that makes us afraid, but a spirit of power and love and self-control.

-And-

Proverbs 3:25-26

You won't be afraid of sudden trouble; you won't fear the ruin that comes to the wicked, because the Lord will keep you safe. He will keep you from being trapped.

Stress is mentally and physically debilitating. The only antidote I know to effectively combat stress is the ability to develop patience. Patience is something many of us lack, and I was especially inpatient when I was younger. With age, I've seemed to become more patient and Psalms 27:14 and 40:1 as well as Romans 15:4-5 provides comforting words to embrace.

Psalm 27:14-40:1

Wait for the Lords help. Be strong and brave and wait for the Lord's help. I waited patiently for the Lord. He turned to me and heard my cry.

-And-

Romans 15: 4-5

Everything that was written in the past was written to teach us. The Scriptures give us patience and encouragement so that we can have hope. Patience and encouragement come from God. And I pray that God will help you all agree with each other the way Christ Jesus wants.

Through Jesus Christ anything is possible and the two key attributes we all need to combat negative and destructive emotions are bravery and strength. **Psalms 31:24 and 27:1-3** delivers a profound message to give us hope:

Psalm 31:24

All you who put hope in the Lord be strong and brave.

-And-

Psalm 27:1-3

The Lord is my light and the one who saves me. I fear no one. The Lord protects my life; I am afraid of no one. If an army surrounds me, I will not be afraid. If war beaks out, I will trust the Lord.

For all of you that have been isolated or quarantined from your family and friends, you must be feeling lonely. Most of us need human contact. A hug, kiss, and the touch of our loved ones. Unfortunately, it doesn't look like we'll be sharing those intimate moments in the very near future. But please, don't despair, remember God is our ultimate companion and He is always there by our side through thick and thin as stated in:

Isaiah 41:10

So, don't worry because I am with you. Don't be afraid, because I am your God. I will make you strong and will help you; I will support you with my right hand that saves you.

-And-

Psalm 46:1

God is our protection and our strength. He always helps in times of trouble.

God never takes a break, He's on call 24/7 and ready to listen and provide comfort whenever you need. God has become my favorite driving companion. I love talking to Him when I'm driving because He's an attentive listener and never tells me how to drive, not like my wife or best friends do. I find time passes quickly and I always arrive at my destination well before finishing my conversations and prayers. This is time well spent as stated in:

1 John 1:13

Our fellowship is with God the Father and with His Son.

Added with the hopeful words of :

Mathew 21:22

If you believe, you will get anything you ask for in prayer.

Finally, depression. Who wouldn't feel a little down in the dumps or be a bit depressed during these troubling times? But once again, **Psalm 34:17 and Isaiah 51:11** remind us there is nothing to be depressed about, because God is there to support us through it all.

Psalm 34:17

The Lord hears good people when they cry out to Him, and He saves them from all their troubles.

-And-

Isaiah 51:11

The people the Lord has freed will return and enter Jerusalem with joy. Their happiness will last forever. They will have joy and gladness, and all sadness and sorrow will be gone far away.

We're not physically together, but it would be nice to try and spiritually connect by reciting the beautiful, meaningful, and timely:

Psalm 23

The Lord is my Shepard, I shall not want, He makes me lie down in green pastures.

He leads me beside still waters; He restores my soul; He leads me down the righteous paths for His name's sake.

Even though I walk through the valley of darkness I will fear no evil for You are with me, Your rod and staff comfort me.

You prepare a table for me in the presence of my enemies, You anoint my head with oil, my cup overflows. Surely goodness and mercy shall follow me all the days of my life, and I shall dwell in the house of the Lord, my whole life long.

Live by the words of:

Romans 8:14

The true children of God are those who let God's Spirit lead them and don't allow yourselves to become overwhelmed with negative emotions. And trust in:

Proverbs 16:3

Depend on the Lord in whatever you do, and your plans will succeed.

Until we can once again be together. Stay safe and healthy and let the scriptures provide you with peace, hope, and comfort. May God's unwavering love and gracious mercy bless you and keep you and your families safe and healthy.

Amen

The Serenity Prayer and Psalm 23 have had incredible positive effects on my life, and I recite them as part of my daily praying ritual.

I also feel moved by God to share these magical words with anyone who I think may be in need of some inspiration, encouragement, peace, hope, and comfort.

Chapter 5
Our Spiritual Connection

My father-in-law Al and I had a very close loving relationship. We enjoyed kidding each other and we spoke literally every day. He'd call me every morning while I was getting ready to go to work and our conversations would continue while I shaved, showered, dressed, and headed out the door.

We talked about everything and anything, from family issues, politics, celebrities, finance, sex, you name it. No topic was off limits. Ironically, the only subjects we never discussed in all our years and conversations was our feelings about God, our religious and spiritual beliefs, and whether we believed in an afterlife. I don't know why, but those subjects just never seemed to come up.

Maybe we were both a bit uncomfortable about bringing it up and honestly, I didn't know anything at the time that would have been worth discussing.

Our family spent the summers on Long Beach Island just five houses from my in-law's home. Every morning, my father-in-law would walk up to our house, typically at the crack of dawn, and yell into the window "You're missing the best part of the day!"

On Wednesday, August 13th, 2008, he walked up to our house on his daily routine, but this day he came up a little bit later, so everyone was gone, and we were alone. He had a peculiar look on his face and was obviously disturbed or upset, so I asked him if there was anything wrong.

I'll never forget our discussion. He confided that he was having unsettling dreams that were causing him to lose sleep, and that the dreams were so real and vivid they seemed more like visions or apparitions.

He explained his wife, Grace, who had passed away 16 years earlier, appeared floating at the foot of his bed just before his regular wake-up time and that he felt she was coming for him.

While my father-in-law's bedroom visions were disturbing and unsettling, he wasn't scared and told me he wasn't afraid. But I knew he was concerned and was questioning if there was some sort of supernatural or deeper spiritual meaning or message behind my mother-in-law's appearances and morning visits.

Psalm 4:8 is a wonderful comforting verse:

I go to bed and sleep in peace, because, Lord, only You keep me safe.

After talking for a while, I confessed I also had some sleeping issues and that I found praying soothed me back into a restful sleep. I told him I prayed for him, all my family and friends and always ended my prayers with the Serenity Prayer followed by the Lord's Prayer. I told him how I had discovered the Serenity Prayer in "Lessons Learned" and as I began to recite those powerful 27 words, he chimed in acknowledging he was familiar with the prayer.

For the first time in our relationship, we discussed God, the possibility of an afterlife and what spirituality meant to each of us. I told him I felt most people wrestled with faith and that I was facing the same challenge of belief and desperately wanted to have a strong faith, but just didn't know how to obtain it.

Our conversation was never planned, but the timing couldn't have been better. My father-in-law was at peace and the Serenity Prayer helped him to surrender his fears over to God.

I also had the unique opportunity to share my inner concerns and aspirations to believe in God and the afterlife. I was able to confess to my dearest confidant my deep heart-felt desire to believe and my need for confirmation.

A few days later, he told me he had taken my advice and had begun praying for all of us and included the Serenity Prayer as a central part of his prayers. My formula apparently worked because he was truly at peace, at ease, and was finally getting some good restful sleep.

Serenity is best expressed in:

Psalm 29:11

The Lord gives strength to His people; the Lord blesses His people with peace.

In hindsight, I think my father-in-law suspected he was going to die soon because he thanked me more than usual, and one day before he died, I remember him saying "Geez Dave, I feel like all I do is thank you for taking care of things."

That same day as he walked up the street, he saw a friend's motorcycle parked outside our house and at age 82, expressed how he'd love to ride a motorcycle.

Psalm 119:165

Those who love Your teachings will find true peace, and nothing will defeat them.

At the time, it just seemed like another one of our many conversations and now we had a new, interesting topic to explore together.

I didn't know it, but this experience with my father-in-law was the beginning of my own personal journey to discovering faith. I believe it was all part of God's greater plan for my father-in-law and me.

I never realized the power of my spoken words. Witnessing the effect my words had on my father-in-law enlightened me and made me realize my words had meaning.

This experience taught me how powerful words can be and the importance of choosing words wisely. I now understood how they can positively or negatively affect those that they are directed to.

Chapter Three of The Book of James is dedicated to the power of your words.

James 3 – Taming the Tongue

Not many of you should become teachers, my brothers, and sisters, for you know that we who teach will be judged with greater strictness. For all of us make many mistakes. Anyone who makes no mistakes in speaking is perfect, able to keep the whole body in check with a bridle. If we put bits into the mouths of horses to make them obey us, we guide their whole bodies. Or look at ships: though they are so large that it takes strong winds to drive them, yet they are guided by a very small rudder wherever the will of the pilot directs. So also, the tongue is a small member, yet it boasts of great exploits. How great a forest is set ablaze by a small fire! And the tongue is a fire. The tongue is placed among our members as a world of inequity; it stains the whole body, sets on fire the cycle of nature, and is itself set on fire by hell. For every species of beast and bird, of reptile and sea creature, can be tamed and has been tamed by the human species, but no one can tame the tongue – a restless evil, full of deadly poison. With it we bless the Lord and Father, and with it we curse those who are made in the likeness of God. From the same mouth come blessings and cursing. My brothers and sisters, this ought not be so. Does a spring pour forth from the same opening both fresh and brackish water? Can a fig tree, my brothers and sisters, yield olives, or a grapevine figs? No more can saltwater yield fresh.

Taming my tongue was one of the most difficult lessons for me to learn and I'm sorry to admit I failed many times over the years. I need to continually remind myself to control my tongue and to use my words to motivate, inspire, and support and to be mindful of how my words can also be destructive, hurtful, and worse, destroy the spirit of those at which they are directed. My conversations with my father-in-law helped me to understand people were really listening to what I had to say and that my words truly had meaning.

Deuteronomy 23:23

Whatever your lips utter you must diligently perform, just as you have freely vowed to the Lord your God with your own mouth.

Words matter, and maybe that's why God gave us two ears and one mouth!

Chapter 6
Wisdom Received

My father-in-law suffered from a horrible driving disease diagnosed by the family as "Terminal Road Rage." He just hated being behind people that didn't know where they were going or who might be out for a simple joy ride.

When he was behind the wheel, he had a specific purpose and mission. Get to Shop Rite, Home Depot or Lowe's and get back home. Even though he was retired for many years and really had nothing but time on his hands, he made his shopping and chores into purposeful, meaningful missions and eliminated any type of dilly-dallying.

His road rage was worse when he wasn't driving but sitting in the passenger seat. Now as the navigator he was free to see everything around him and bark orders like, "don't let him in" or "beat her before the light changes."

Ecclesiastes 7:9

Don't become angry quickly, because getting angry is foolish.

Well, there was a traffic light where cars would always jockey for position to turn left off the island. As we'd approach the light you could feel the tension building up in the car and when we were within 250 yards of the light his blood pressure would rise, and with smoke blowing out of his ears he'd start yelling, "they don't know there's two lanes, come on, come on, look at that, what did I tell you, we're going to miss the turn, the light is changing, don't let them in, come on."

Proverbs 16:32 tells us:

Patient people have great understanding, but people with quick tempers show their foolishness.

So, with that in mind, I'd slow down, and say the same thing back every time, "so what's the rush, do you have an important appointment we're going to miss? Take it easy, life's too short, we have all day, enjoy yourself."

Proverbs 15:1

A gentle answer will calm a person's anger, but an unkind answer will cause more anger.

The fact that we would travel to Shop Rite, Home Depot or Lowe's at least twice a week for years meant we had this same conversation a hundred times over. It was as though our driving trips were all scripted. Approaching the light … begin the dialogue … make the turn.

On August 16, 2008, we were off for our traditional bi-weekly run to Home Depot. But something was very, very different. As we approached the light that normally made his blood pressure rise, he said nothing. As we waited at the light for all the unknowledgeable and inexperienced drivers to pass and not let us through, he looked at me and said, "Are you proud of me?", and I said, "Yes, I am," He asked, "Do you know why you're proud of me?" "Yes" I said, "you're finally learning."

John 14:27

I leave you peace; My peace I give you. I do not give it to you as the world does. So, don't let your hearts be troubled or afraid.

My father-in-law was calm, patient, in total control and not agitated by the traffic or poor drivers in any way and seemed to truly be at complete peace.

Proverbs 14:16-17

Wise people are careful and stay out of trouble, but fools are careless and quick to act. Someone with a quick temper does foolish things, but someone with the understanding remain calm.

That was the last time we ever drove together and at that moment, I didn't realize or understand the significance of his actions. In retrospect, he was finally at total peace. Somehow, he saw the bigger picture of life and was at ease with what was to come.

His unexplainable transformation was initially puzzling to me. Then I realized he was praying and reciting the Serenity Prayer. It's not that he knew he was going to die, he just stopped worrying about the things he had no control over, and he finally learned how to accept the gift of surrender. God had given him the wisdom. As for me, our last drive confirmed the incredible power of the Serenity Prayer.

Philippians 4:6-7

Do not worry about anything, but pray and ask God for everything you need, always giving thanks. And God's peace, which is so great we cannot understand it, will keep your hearts and minds in Christ Jesus.

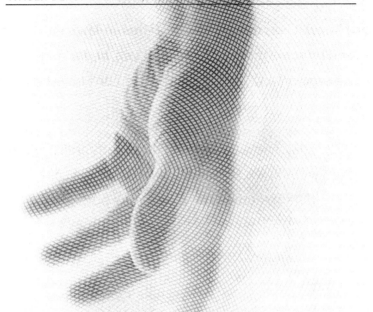

Chapter 7
No Such Thing as Coincidence

We didn't know it was going to be my father-in-law's last hours with us, and by some miraculous state of fate, his last night was the perfect send off and saying goodbye couldn't have been better planned.

As a believer today, I now understand these extraordinary events and the sequences in which they occurred were not coincidences, but Gods' pre-determined master plan for the both of us.

Judges 18:6

The priest replied, "Go in peace. The mission you are on is under the eye of the Lord."

The first event involved my wife Jody, my daughter Jessica, and then future husband Mike. Jessica and Mike had rented a home with friends about an hour away in a different Jersey shore town and hadn't visited us all summer. While we normally always find time to get together, this summer was especially peculiar. The summer season was almost over, and we just never had a chance to see each other. Well, for some strange reason, Jessica and Mike decided to surprise us and came to our shore house for an overnight visit. My father-in-law hadn't seen Jessie for months and was absolutely thrilled to see her and Mike.

The second remarkable event happened minutes later when my son Kristofer and his wife Sue arrived. It wasn't unusual for Kris and Sue to come down the shore each weekend, but it was highly unusual for them to arrive so early in the day. Sue's busiest day at the salon where she worked was always Saturday and they normally never made it down until late evening after my father-in-law had already gone to bed.

But on this bizarre day, Sue went to work and learned there had been a scheduling error. This was the first time she didn't have any afternoon client appointments, so Kris and Sue came down the shore earlier than expected.

The third strange event was the arrival of my father-in-law's favorite neighbors Denny and Rene who had moved to Florida, He loved this couple and considered them family. Their homes on the island were literally right next to each other, separated by only an eight-foot-wide driveway. They would converse all day through their kitchen windows, talking about everything from recipes to up to the minute political commentary. They always included my father-in-law in all their parties, and he really enjoyed their company and spending crazy times together. He was happy for them when they built a home just two blocks away on the bay, but also saddened by the logistical separation. Denny and Rene continued to invite him whenever they had a party or get-together and frequently came by to check in.

John 15:12-15

"This is my commandment, that you love one another as I have loved you. No one has greater love than this, to lay down one's life for one's friend. You are my friends if you do what I command

you. I do not call you servants any longer, because the servant does not know what the master is doing; but I have called you friends, because I have made known to you everything that I have heard from my Father.

After a few years of living on the bay, Denny and Rene retired and moved to Florida. My father-in-law really missed their company and knew there would be only rare opportunities to see them again.

Psalm 139:16

Your eyes behold my unformed substance. In your book were written all the days that was formed for me, when none of them as yet existed.

Well, as my father-in-law's destiny would have it, Denny, and Rene had just come back from Florida that same day to attend a friend's wedding and rented their original home eight feet across the driveway from my father-in-law's house.

The fourth phenomenal event in this bizarre series of coincidences included the presence of two of our very close couples John and Val, and Mike and Kathy. Jody and I always celebrated the best and happiest of times with them and we could always count on them to support us during the saddest and most stressful of times.

Proverbs 27:10

Do not forsake your friend or the friend of your parents; do not go to the house of your kindred in the day of your calamity. Better is a neighbor who is nearby than kindred who are far away.

My father-in-law appreciated the sincere friendships we have, and he also enjoyed their company and loved them as though they were family. What added to making this a peculiar event was the fact this was the first time in all the years we owned our house that both neighbors on each side of us decided to rent out their homes. And as chance would have it, John and Val rented the house on one side and Mike and Kathy rented the house on the other side.

Because of everyone's schedules constantly changing neither couple was able to come down the shore at the same time, except on this specific day. My immediate family, Jody, Kris, Sue, Jessica, Mike, and our extended family John, Val, Mike, Kathy, Denny, and Rene, were all together with my father-in-law on a spectacular Saturday afternoon at the Jersey shore.

Ecclesiastes 10:19

Feasts are made for laughter; wine gladdens life, and money meets every need.

The only thing that can be anticipated or foretold when we're all together is that a big party will ensue. As expected, we began cooking and barbequing in the connecting backyards and as night fell, we lit the tiki torches, ate, drank, sang, and danced to music from the 50's through the 90's. As the festivities continued, other neighbors began coming over to party with us. Our little get-together soon became a block party and the feast, unbeknownst to me at the time, was to be my father-in-law's final tribute and farewell party. This was the fifth unexplainable event to occur that night.

Deuteronomy 14:26

Spend the money for whatever you wish – oxen, sheep, wine, strong drink or whatever you desire. And you shall eat there in the presence of the Lord your God, you and your household rejoicing together.

My father-in-law was very well known by most of the residents and seasonal renters on 17th Street and everyone referred to him as "the mayor of 17th Street." As they'd walk past his house on their way to the beach, he'd wave and strike up a conversation about anything you'd imagine. He was very well liked and more importantly, well respected. Everyone knew they could rely on Al to lend them a helping hand or ladder since he was the only one on the block with tools, and who knew how to use them. He was also a person who unselfishly spent a lifetime helping and supporting others.

Psalm 13:3

Consider and answer me O Lord my God! Give light to my eyes, or I will sleep the sleep of death.

I remember looking at him that night and feeling an overwhelming sense of happiness. He seemed to be in all his glory, his face was lit up with an expression of pure joy, and his eyes twinkled and shined as he watched everyone he loved enjoying the festivities.

Isaiah 35:10 – Crown of Happiness

And the ransomed of the Lord shall return, and come to Zion with singing; everlasting joy shall be upon their heads; they shall obtain joy and gladness, and sorrow and sighing shall flee away.

The sixth peculiar event of the evening was the time at which my father-in-law left the party to go home.

Typically, he'd walk home just before 8:00 PM so he could watch Bill O'Reilly, one of his favorite talk show hosts on Fox Cable News. But on this rare night, he stayed till nearly 12:00 AM and as everyone else remained outside in the backyard he, Kris and I were alone in our small bungalow living room. Kris and I were joking with him about a woman at the party who was openly flirting with him. We kept kidding him that she obviously wanted him, and he laughed out loud and said, "forget it, I don't even think about it anymore." Three generations busting each other and being able to enjoy each others humor was truly a special and unforgettable moment. Unbeknownst to any of us at the time, this was literally his farewell party, and by the next morning our world would change forever.

James 4:13-16 No Certainty of Tomorrow

Come now, you who say, "Today or tomorrow we will go to such and such a town and spend a year there, doing business and making money." Yet you do not even know what tomorrow will bring. What is your life? For you are a mist that appears for a little while and then vanishes. Instead, you ought to say, "If the Lord wishes, we will live and do this or that." As it is, you boast in your arrogance; all such boasting is evil.

At the time, I felt all of these crazy events were just coincidences. But now I'm convinced there is no such thing as coincidences. God has a master plan for each of us and I try to be alert and recognize the opportunities He puts before me. More importantly, I willingly accept and appreciate His guidance and direction.

Romans 8:14

The true children of God are those who let God's Spirit guide them.

Chapter 8
Butterflies and Superstitions

Christians associate butterflies with the resurrection of Jesus Christ and the symbol of the butterfly is commonly used during the holiest of Christian celebrations, Easter. Butterflies are insects and considered to die as a caterpillar, get buried in a cocoon and then are reborn and transition into a beautiful new life as a butterfly. Butterflies represent a re-birth and transformation in faith.

Acts 13:32-33

And we bring you the good news that what God promised to our ancestors He has fulfilled for us, their children, by raising Jesus; as also it is written in the second Psalm, "You are my Son; today I have begotten you."

There is no mention of butterflies in the bible and no scripture can be directly referenced to butterflies. However, there is plenty written about faith and the resurrection which is symbolized by butterflies.

Butterflies are the most common and frequently mentioned ADC (After Death Communication) sign and are universally associated with our souls by many different religions, spiritual followers, and cultures.

They have a significant meaning of hope, change, endurance, transformation, and life. Butterflies are spiritual symbols for life after death.

Hebrews 11:3

It is by faith we understand that the whole world was made by God's command so what we see was made by something that cannot be seen.

Growing up I never heard of any stories about butterflies or rainbows or birds or anything being communication conduits to loved ones that died.

As a youth, I heard "Old Italian" superstitions like if a bird flew in your house, someone close to you was going to die. At the age of 13, I found a black bird flying around in the completely sealed basement of our home. My father opened the basement windows, and the bird eventually flew out. We never figured out how that bird entered the house, but a few weeks later, my grandmother, who I was very close to, died. Back then I viewed this as a pure coincidence because no sane person would put credibility into an "Old Italian" wise tale.

Another silly superstition I heard as a youth was that if dreamt your teeth were loose or falling out, someone close was also going to die. Unfortunately, I've been grinding my teeth ever since I heard this one!

But the first time I heard about butterflies being a form of an ADC was a few months following the death of my daughter-in-law Sue's father, Fred. He died in his sleep of a massive heart attack 17 months before my father-in-law passed.

Fred and Al were very similar. Both were wonderful and generous retired men who enjoyed meeting and talking with people. At one point, they lived blocks away from each other in Irvington, New Jersey, and had a real connection whenever we all got together.

Like my father-in-law, Fred never complained about aches or pains, and except for a hernia operation he put off, Fred was strong and in relatively good health. He rarely visited a doctor, but on Friday, March 30, 2007, he felt terrible and went to a local walk-in urgent care medical center. They diagnosed him with either a bad cold or flu, gave him antibiotics, and sent him home with instructions to rest. Fred fell asleep that night on his couch in the family room and never woke up.

Fred's sudden death on March 31, 2007, left Sue and her mother Marilyn feeling cheated since they didn't have the opportunity to say goodbye. Both were seeking closure, so a few months after his death, they visited a medium to see if there was any way to satisfy this void.

Sue and Marilyn made an appointment with a medium using only their first names. They recorded their individual sessions, and I was shocked after hearing the audio. The medium provided intimate private facts, dates, and statements that only Fred, Marilyn, Sue, and our family would have known.

I was always a fairly jaded guy and believed these mediums were quacks and imposters, out to make a fast buck on the weak, distraught, and broken hearted. While I think it's still smart to be skeptical, I must admit Sue and her mother Marilyn both experienced a tremendous healing benefit and closure that they so desperately needed.

They accepted Fred's passing and felt a spiritual awakening and enlightenment after their sessions with the medium. It was as if someone flicked on a light switch and they both had a renewed interest in their faith and belief in God and an afterlife.

Zechariah 10:2

For the teraphim utter nonsense, and the diviners sees lies; the dreamers tell false dreams and give empty consolation. Therefore, the people wander like sheep; they suffer for lack of a Shepard.

Sue and her mother were the first people I talked to about butterflies and how they relate to communicating with those who have died. The medium told them during their separate sessions that Fred's spirit would appear to them in the form of a butterfly, and he would also try to communicate or contact them by turning the lights in their houses off and on.

Since then, we've all witnessed unexplainable flickering of lights, as well as the doorbell sporadically ringing when the entire family is gathered together. And yes, as you can imagine, everyone began seeing butterflies more often and have become much more aware of their physical presence.

These events aren't scary or creepy in any way. They're entertaining, and we acknowledge Fred's presence and typically say, "Hey Fred what's going on … thanks for watching over us."

However, at the time I was still very skeptical about the meaning behind these butterfly sightings.

My lack of knowledge or belief made it difficult for me to accept them as an ADC and I didn't place much credibility into their presence.

But my belief in butterflies was about to start changing over the next few days.

Romans 12:2

Do not be conformed to this world, "but be transformed by the renewing of your minds, so that you may discern what is the will of God – what is good and acceptable and perfect."

Chapter 9
Beginning with no End

Mark 3:21

When His family heard it, they went out to restrain Him, for people were saying "He has gone out of His mind."

Both of our children were grown and out of the house when we decided to get a dog. We brought our beautiful Bearded Collie puppy, named Romeo, to the shore house and when my father-in-law saw him for the first time, he couldn't help telling us we were crazy!!!

Ecclesiastes 4:9-10

Two are better than one, because they have a good reward for their toil. For if they fall, one will lift the other; but woe to one who is alone and falls and does not have another to help.

He couldn't understand why we would get a dog, since our kids were all grown, and we finally had freedom. Well, in no time he fell in love with Romeo.

A year later, we got Romeo a companion who we named Juliet. Now my father-in-law really thought we were nuts. But he loved Romeo sitting at his feet and laughed and giggled like a school boy as Juliet simultaneously climbed all over his body, kissing and licking him like he was covered in sugar.

My father-in-law finally admitted two dogs were a joyful idea and he understood they would keep each other company. He was the first to offer watching them when we went away, and he'd use visiting us as an excuse to spend time with Romeo and Juliet.

They never acted differently to my father-in-law from when they were eight-pound puppies to Romeo, who was now at a robust 82 pounds, and Juliet an agile 42 pounds.

Romeo always sat on top of his feet and Juliet would jump up on his lap and start kissing him from head to toe before she'd curl up around his neck like a cat. He loved the unquestionable affection, but as much as Romeo loved him, he would never, under any circumstance, go to my father-in-law's house.

Leviticus 26:36

… the sound of a driven leaf shall put them to flight, and they shall flee as one flees from the sword, and they shall fall though no one pursues.

You see, Bearded Collies are quirky characters and can be easily spooked. When Romeo was a puppy, he was traumatized by the loud chime from an antique French clock that hung on a wall in my father-in-law's family room. While visiting one day, the chime sounded and surprised Romeo who darted for the door like a nuclear explosion went off. From that day on, we could never get Romeo to even approach my father-in-law's property line.

Romeo and Juliet were inseparable, and we always walked them together. Because of Romeo's anxiety, Juliet never had an opportunity to visit my father-in-law's home even though we were only six houses from each other.

He lived on our right side toward the ocean, and we resided left of his home toward the bay.

When we'd walk the dogs, Romeo would plant all 82 pounds and turn frantically left toward the bay. There was nothing we could do to steer him in the direction of the ocean and my father-in-law's home. The only way we could walk him toward the ocean was to walk west (left) toward the bay then at the end of the block turn either right or left and take the adjacent block straight east toward the ocean.

It was wonderful having John and Val and Mike and Kathy renting homes on both sides of ours. John and Val also had two Bearded Collies named Rocky and Belle. August 17th, the day after the block party, was a spectacular Sunday morning and a perfect day to play tennis with my friends.

First Butterfly Sighting

I was just about to serve, when out of the corner of my eye I saw a big, beautiful orange, red and black Monarch butterfly that landed literally inches from my left foot.

Stopping in mid-serve, I gently picked the motionless butterfly up in my right hand and carried it off, placing it softly on the side of the tennis court, away from play.

To my surprise, this beautiful butterfly that seemed nearly lifeless followed me back to the service line. I instinctively opened the palm of my right hand, and the multi-colored butterfly flew directly toward me and landed in the palm of my hand. I'll never forget whispering quietly under my breath, "Hi Fred, thanks for watching over us," and then lifted the butterfly into the air as it slowly flew off.

John 3:3

Jesus answered him, "Very truly I tell you, no one can see the kingdom of God without being born from above."

Soon after the butterfly appeared, a sudden feeling of complete exhaustion came over me. I had to leave the tennis courts and went straight home which was only a few blocks away.

Just as I got home, Kathy came over for morning coffee. She told me the makeshift fence we built to contain the dogs was knocked down and Juliet was missing.

Second Butterfly Sighting

As I ran into the backyard, I saw three pure white, large white large butterflies hovering over the downed fence exactly where Juliet had obviously escaped from. I was frantic and all I could think of was Juliet running in the street and getting hit by a car.

My instinct was to run immediately left toward the bay. I was only about five houses toward the bay screaming her name when my buddy Mike yelled out he had her. I looked down the street toward the ocean, and there was Mike holding Juliet by the collar about ten feet from my father-in-law's driveway. This was a weird event, but something even stranger was Juliet seemed to be heading directly to see my father-in-law who had missed his morning coffee with us and unbeknownst to me was home alone, and in pain.

Psalm 103:1-20

Of David. Bless the Lord, O my soul, and all that is within me, bless His holy name. Bless the Lord, O my soul, and forget not all His benefits, who forgives all your iniquity, who heals all your diseases, who redeems your life from the Pit, who crowns you with steadfast love and mercy, who satisfies you with good as long as you live so that your youth is renewed like the eagle's.

In all the confusion, I didn't notice my wife Jody was already in her car preparing to take her father to the hospital. She told me he had a pain in his side and lower back and felt she needed to take him to the hospital to be checked out. I followed her to my father-in-law's home where he was sitting uncomfortably on the couch.

I quickly checked him over and asked if they wanted me to go with them. But they both felt it was just a precautionary visit, and that it felt like a kidney or gall stone or maybe just a severe gas pocket. They wanted me to stay with our friends who had come down the shore to be with us.

Job 30:17

The night racks my bones, and the pain that gnaws me takes no rest.

About a half-an-hour later Jody called me from the hospital and said her father was in a lot of pain and he hadn't been seen yet. I immediately drove to the hospital, arriving only 15 minutes after her call.

He had just been brought into the emergency room, but still hadn't been examined by a doctor yet. My father-in-law was in extreme pain at this point, and it was now generating in his back. We still thought it might be a gall stone or kidney stone, but the pain was quickly increasing.

I went to the front desk and told the scheduling nurse that my father-in-law had an abdominal aortic aneurysm that we had been monitoring and he needed to be seen immediately. Al was a World

War II medic who, while administering to others on a beach in the South Pacific, was hit himself and carried shrapnel metal in him since 1946. This was one tough guy who was experiencing tremendous, intense pain. A nurse finally brought him for a CAT scan. Within minutes he returned with the head ER doctor who informed us that my father-in-law was in a critical state because his aorta aneurism, had ruptured, and a vascular surgeon was on the way.

While we were aware of the aneurism, the fact that it ruptured was a complete shock.

We had been monitoring his condition for years and only five weeks earlier, his vascular specialist from a well-respected Northern New Jersey hospital performed a 3D CAT scan to monitor and measure the size of the aneurysm. After repeated calls to his doctor's office to find out the results, the doctor's receptionist finally told my father-in-law not to worry. She explained that if anything was wrong the doctor certainly would've contacted him already and that "No news was good news." These were literally her "final last words."

Jeremiah 8:11

They have treated the wound of my people carelessly, saying "Peace, peace," when there is no peace.

So being told by the emergency room doctors that the aneurysm had ruptured was beyond our comprehension. Knowing time was working against us, the vascular surgeon consulting with us in the ER looked my father-in-law directly in the eye and said, "This is very difficult for me to say, and will be more difficult for you to hear, but in my opinion, you are going to die from this condition, and you will probably die today." Then he looked at us and said, "Why haven't you taken care of this, why did you let it go this far?"

Mark 5:25-26

Now there was a woman who had been suffering from hemorrhages for twelve years. She had endured much under many physicians and had spent all that she had; and she was no better, but rather grew worse.

I felt as if a knife was thrust into my heart since I was the one who had been taking him to the vascular specialist in Northern New Jersey for years and felt personally responsible for monitoring his condition and well-being.

Ezekiel 7:26

Disaster comes upon disaster, rumor follows rumor; they shall keep seeking a vision from the prophet; instruction shall perish from the priest and counsel from the elders.

I called the office of his North Jersey vascular specialist from the emergency room and after explaining the critical situation, was told a covering doctor would immediately call me back. Within minutes, a covering doctor called and confirmed the findings of the 3D CAT scan taken just weeks before. He also asked why we hadn't taken care of this sooner and told me my father-in-law was a walking time bomb ready to explode. He was also surprised to learn the doctor he was covering for had never called my father-in-law or us with the results of his scan, and that we were told "No news is good news." There was a long pause on the other end of the phone, dead silence as the covering doctor tried to compose himself. He instructed me to listen to the ER vascular surgeon, that this was a critical situation and to do whatever he recommends because we probably don't have many options. I then gave the phone to the vascular surgeon in the ER who spoke to the covering doctor for just a minute then redirected his attention back to us.

The ER team worked feverishly to keep my father-in-law comfortable and stable while the vascular surgeon explained our extremely limited options, complicated by the fact he was taking blood thinners for an erratic heartbeat.

Joel 3:14

Multitudes, multitudes, in the valley of decision! For the day of the Lord is near in the valley of decision.

The first option was to operate at this Southern New Jersey hospital, but they didn't have the proper size grafts, nor the proper bypass equipment required to perform such a complicated surgery. He told us that if he was to attempt the surgery my father-in-law would more than likely die on the operating table.

Our second option was trying to stabilize him for a helicopter flight and locating a vascular team of surgeons and a hospital willing to accept him for this surgery. Even if all went well and they were able to locate a team and a hospital, my father-in-law's chances of survival were less than 10%.

The third option was to do nothing. Make him comfortable and let him die, right there in the ER.

My father-in-law looked at Jody, her elder sister, Allyn, and younger sister, Kristine, and me and said, "I never imagined it would end like this," as he did his best to stay composed and comprehend the magnitude of his situation.

We all looked at each other and then he said ,"Well, OK let's go for it."

Jody and I, my sister-in-laws, Kristine's boyfriend Bob, and granddaughter Bryan Lee each had an opportunity to express our love and try to give him a sense of optimism and hope for his forth coming procedure and ordeal.

Jeremiah 17:14

Lord, heal me, and I will truly be healed. Save me, and I will truly be saved. You are the one I praise.

About a half hour later the ER vascular surgeon found a team and hospital within a helicopter ride willing to accept my father-in-law's case. Looking back, I think he was testing option number 3 and waiting for what he believed to be the inevitable. But my father-in-law was a tough guy, a real fighter and had somehow become stable enough for flight and transport.

A vascular team at the University of Pennsylvania Hospital was willing to operate on him at the age of 82 and were already preparing for his arrival. We soon heard the engines and rotating blades of a helicopter and two medic-vac pilots in full uniform came charging into the ER and took over for the ER personnel. Within minutes, they had my father-in-law strapped into a stretcher and as they wheeled him to the helicopter for transport, we had a short opportunity to speak with him individually.

He said to me, "Dave, take care of the girls." I told him "Don't worry, I will." As I fought back the tears, I did my best to encourage him to keep on fighting, not to give up and that I loved him. It was an incredibly heart breaking and emotional moment as he replied, "I love you Dave."

These were his last verbally spoken words to me, but most certainly not his final communication.

We all stood motionless looking toward the sky as the helicopter flew off into the horizon. Our only thoughts were that this may be the last time we would ever see him alive.

Proverbs 12:25

Anxiety weighs down the human heart, but a good word cheers it up.

There was an irony about my father-in-law flying off in the helicopter as a patient. The helicopter pilot asked if he had ever flown in a heli-copter. He replied, not since he was in the service during World War II. He was a marine medic taking care of the wounded until he was wounded himself by shrapnel as he mended marines on a beach in the South Pacific.

He was the ultimate caregiver and committed his life to helping oth-ers. He was a Captain on the Newark Fire Department, putting himself in danger every day to save the lives of people he didn't know. My mother-in-law, Grace, suffered a lifetime from crippling and debilitating arthritis before she died. So, at the youthful age of 52, he retired devot-ing himself to caring for her. Many years after her passing, my father-in-law met a woman who became his companion. She had a 40-year-old single daughter who had a brain aneurysm rupture behind her eye. That rupture rendered her legally blind with brain damage and severe memory loss. He once again cared for both his 84-year-old companion, and her permanently disabled middle-aged daughter.

Third Butterfly Sighting

Earlier that morning, Kristofer took Sue, Jessica, and Mike on his boat for a cruise to Atlantic City.

They were having lunch at an outdoor restaurant on the boardwalk of Atlantic City overlooking the Atlantic Ocean when I called to break the sad news of his grandfather's condition.

As I was explaining to him what was happening, I overheard Sue say, "Hi Dad." At that precise moment, a large orange, red and black Monarch butterfly flew to the table where they were dining. This butterfly remained hovering and landed on the table during the entire time they were having lunch.

I told Kris not to tell the others because I didn't want them to panic, but to come home as soon as possible. Not to alarm them, he made an excuse about his boat, and they all quickly left to return to LBI.

The ocean had turned choppy and rough, so the trip back to the island was difficult and very uncomfortable. Their return should have taken much longer in those weather conditions, but Kris was able to navigate it back in record time. They returned just in time for all of us to leave Long Beach Island together and travel to the University of Pennsylvania Hospital where Pop-Pop Al was flown for an emergency operation to save his life.

1 Corinthians 15:50-58

What I am saying, brothers and sisters, is this: flesh blood cannot inherit the kingdom of God, nor does the perishable inherit the imperishable. Listen, I will tell you a mystery! We will not all die, but we will all be changed, in a moment, in the twinkling of an eye, at the last trumpet. For the trumpet will sound, and the dead will be raised imperishable, and we will be changed. For this perishable body must put on imperishability, and this mortal body must put on immortality. When this perishable body puts on imperishability, and this mortal body puts on immortality then the saying that is written will be fulfilled: "Death has been swallowed up in victory." "Where, O death is your victory? Where, O death is your sting?" The sting of death is sin, and the power of sin is the law. But thanks be to God, who gives us the victory through our Lord Jesus Christ. Therefore, my beloved, be steadfast, immovable, always excelling in the work of the Lord, because you know that in the Lord your labor is not in vain.

While it would take only about 20 minutes for the helicopter to arrive at the University of Pennsylvania hospital, it was going to take us more than a few hours to get the immediate family together and drive the 100 plus miles to be with him. We all arrived together at the hospital in the mid-afternoon and sat in the waiting room of the Rhoads Wing until the early hours of the morning. Several doctors and nurses kept us apprised of the progress and gave us the operation's status.

Finally, at about 4:30 AM on August 18, 2008, the senior vascular surgeon who led the team operating on my father-in-law came into the waiting room and consulted with the entire family.

He explained they resuscitated him twice in the helicopter on the way to the University of Pennsylvania hospital. Once there, they gave him several blood transfusions and medications to clot his thin blood and stabilize him for the operation.

The surgeon told us the operation was a success and that they had repaired one large aneurysm on his aorta, but didn't operate on a second located lower into the stomach. He felt my father-in-law had been through a lot and they could address the other less critical aneurysm down the road.

Then he asked the question we had already heard twice just hours before. Didn't we know he had an aneurysm and if so, why didn't we take care of it before this? For the third time that day I explained we had been monitoring it and that his doctor never got back to him with the results. My father-in-law had called his North Jersey vascular specialist several times but was told the doctor was on vacation. The receptionist finally told him, "no news is good news." The surgeon's expression said it all. Obviously, he felt the doctor treating my father-in-law had made a very horrible mistake. Afraid we might consider legal action in the future, he quickly changed the subject to the immediate present situation.

He told us my father-in-law stood a good chance of survival and that his prognosis was good, especially for his age and physical condition.

1 Corinthians 12:14

And God raised the Lord and will also raise us by His power.

It was a surreal moment of time. Everyone my father-in-law loved the most was with him in the Intensive Care Recovery Unit in the Rhoads Wing. Each of us had an opportunity and our own special moment with him before leaving to drive the 100 plus miles back home to Long Beach Island.

It was about 7:00 AM when we finally arrived home to the worried waiting arms of our closest friends John, Val, Mike, and Kathy. After talking together for only a few minutes we fell asleep totally exhausted. After sleeping for only about 30 minutes my cell phone rang and it was a nurse from the Rhoads Wing Intensive Care Unit.

She said my father-in-law was on total life support, and we should get there as soon as possible. His condition had worsened, but they could keep him stabilized until we arrived. Being sleep deprived made this gut wrenching news even more difficult to handle. Since there really was nothing anyone could do, I took only Jody, Allyn and Kristine and we immediately drove back to the University of Pennsylvania hospital.

We were very optimistic just a few hours before. Now we had to face the realistic news and begin to prepare ourselves for the worst. A senior attending physician greeted us as we entered the Rhoads Wing, and he immediately took us to see my father-in-law. We were there only a few minutes when his 84-year-old lady companion and her daughter came into the room. We were all shocked by their presence and the doctor, realizing our surprise, brought us to a private conference room to discuss the grave condition.

The physician had an excellent bedside manner. He was sincere and compassionate as he delivered the in-depth details and sad news regarding my father-in-law's current condition and future prognosis.

If my father-in-law survived, he would more than likely be on dialysis for months or possibly for the rest of his life. He also explained he may be confined to a wheelchair, would need PT and OT to learn how to speak again, and there was a good chance he'd require 24/7 personal assistance.

Romans 8:18

I consider that the sufferings of the present time are not worth comparing with the glory about to be revealed to us.

The doctor knew my father-in-law had a medical directive and according to this document, he did not want life support or resuscitation if his quality of life was going to be compromised.

I left Jody and her sisters with the doctor, and I went back to my father-in-law's room to check on his visitors. Standing at the foot of his bed, I just stared at him, wondering if he knew what was going on or if he could hear me. Suddenly, he opened his eyes and looked directly at me. I yelled, "Pop," the name I always called him, and he opened his soft, gray-blue eyes even wider.

I ran to the conference room and told Jody and her sisters to hurry up and come, that their father just opened his eyes. The doctor dismissed his action as an involuntary muscular event and said it was impossible for my father-in-law to communicate with us. Nonetheless, we all ran to his room and his eyes were still open. He was frantically and with determination trying to remove the tubes that were keeping him alive.

We asked his companion and her daughter to leave as the doctors settled my father-in-law down. He began to relax and closed his eyes again.

Now we were really confused. Even though the doctor told us his motions were merely involuntary post-operative muscle movements, he was showing us signs of something more.

Proverbs 6:13

Winking the eyes, shuffling the feet, pointing the fingers.

As soon as the doctors and nurses left the room, he once again opened his eyes and stared directly at us. He gave us the cut signal, moving his right hand across his neck and then trying to pull the breathing tube from his throat. We all tried to stop him and make him relax. I then asked him, "Pop, blink once for yes, two for no. Do you want us to remove the breathing tube and your life support?" He slowly blinked his eyes one time. Then I asked again, "Pop, are you sure you want us to take you off the life support systems?" His next action was astonishing and left no question as to what we were to do. While holding my hand, he pulled himself up to a sitting position in the hospital bed, squeezed my hand until it hurt, looked me straight in the eye and then closed both his eyes as tight and hard as he could and held that position for more than a few seconds before opening them as wide as he possibly could.

I patted him on the chest and said, "Ok Pop, we'll do what you want, I promise. Relax we'll honor your wishes." He slowly laid back down in the bed and closed his eyes for the last time.

Psalm 89:48

What person alive will not die? Who can escape the grave?

Jody, Allyn, Kristine, and I looked at each other in total amazement and acknowledged to one another what we had just witnessed. The doctors told us it was impossible for him to communicate, but we had absolutely no doubt what my father-in-law was telling us.

He was fully aware of his condition and knew exactly what was going on. Being a caregiver his entire life, he understood how difficult this decision was to make, so he made it for us.

We summoned the doctor who had been consulting us and gave him the decision to remove all life support systems. He was once again, very kind and supportive. While it wasn't proper and possibly even unethical to give his own opinion, he told us we were doing the right thing and supported our decision 100%.

We left the room for only a few moments as the doctors and nurses removed all the tubes and life support apparatus that was keeping him alive. After the doctor told us what to expect, they all left us alone in the room, so we could spend those last precious moments with him. As we held his hands and stroked his wavy gray-blond hair we recited the Serenity Prayer and Our Lord's Prayer together. Each breath became a bit shallower and shallower until his last was taken.

James 5:15

The prayer of faith will save the sick, and the Lord will raise them up; and anyone who has committed sins will be forgiven.

On August 18, 2008, at 2:18 PM, my father-in-law, my confidant and best friend, died. I thought nothing of it at the time, but my wife's birthday is 2-18. Numbers that would later in my spiritual journal provide me with meaningful signs and confirmations.

While we were at the hospital, our friends John and Mike were caring for our dogs and at approximately the moment my father-in-law took his last breath they were preparing to take Romeo and Juliet for a walk. Just as they opened the front door, Romeo reacted in a very strange and mysterious way. He bolted out of the house and headed straight toward my father-in-law's house, dragging Mike behind him.

Romeo literally knocked Mike off his feet and Mike did everything he could just to hold on to him. This was totally out of character and an incredible event since everyone knew Romeo's greatest fear was my father-in-law's house. He was defiant, indignant and nothing was going to stop that dog from getting to my father-in-law's home.

We couldn't see, hear, touch, smell, or taste anything that would have identified my father-in-law's health problem. None of our key senses were sharp enough to suspect he was in danger. But obviously Romeo's keen senses recognized he was in grave danger and in need of immediate help or comfort. About a year later, I took Romeo and Juliet to the veterinarian for their annual physicals. I was looking at all the posters on the wall when I spotted this writing:

"An animal's senses are much keener than that of humans. They can see, hear, smell, touch and probably taste with a much higher degree of sensitivity than we can. They seem to have an uncanny ability to sense the coming of a storm, imminent danger or emergency and maybe the ability to recognize presence of spirits."

I believe innocent young children and animals do have a unique ability to sense things that we can't, and these events contribute to my unwavering faith.

Before driving back to Long Beach Island, Jody, Allyn, Kristine, and I stopped for coffee and tried to comprehend and accept what had just happened. Praying together over my father-in-law as he took his last breath helped and gave us a small sense of peace.

We didn't say a word for the entire hour and half ride back to Long Beach Island. We were mentally and physically exhausted, but knew we had a long day of planning my father-in-law's funeral ahead of ourselves.

After making the arrangements at the funeral parlor and cemetery, we went to the Hearthside restaurant to make the re-pass arrangements. This was one of my father-in-law's favorite restaurants and as we were leaving, we heard blaring loud music coming from a plumbing van that was just at that precise moment stopping at a red light directly in front of us. On the side of the van in big white letters was the company's name ... Rhoads. The same name as the intensive care unit at the University of Pennsylvania Hospital where my father-in-law was treated and died.

We all looked at each other and said I guess he agrees with our choice.

Fourth Butterfly Sighting

As the funeral procession drove into the cemetery, a grounds keeper directed me to park our car on a grassy area behind several head stones.

As we slowly drove to the spot where we were instructed to park, everyone in the car went silent. We parked directly behind the back of a very large gray and black granite butterfly.

There was no time to examine the granite butterfly during the burial but on the one-year anniversary of his passing Jody and I went back to visit the cemetery. I was instantly drawn to the large memorable granite butterfly. I read the inscription on the headstone, and it was for a young girl named Olivia.

My friend and creative collaborator Leo Montes de Oca's wife, Deanna, had just given birth to their first child and named her Olivia. It was as if my father-in-law was sending me a message to continue with my book project.

Fifth Butterfly Sighting

Kathy G. worked in my company's accounting department and had an office directly across the hall from mine. We worked together for years and had constant daily contact. Her father died on November 16th, 2009, a little more than a year after my father-in-law. She had just come back to work from her bereavement time off, so I went into her office to check on her and ask if there was anything she needed.

We were sitting in her office talking about her father's untimely passing and she told me an incredible story about her six-year-old son insisting on calling her father the Saturday before he died. Her son was adamant and took it upon himself to make the call and speak to her father.

As she was talking, I found myself gazing at the pictures and knick-knacks in her room. I stopped listening and couldn't hear a word she was saying. Kathy was speaking and her lips were moving, but

I was frozen. Everywhere I looked I saw butterflies. She had pictures, drawings, wedding favors and statues of butterflies in her office. I literally became numb and asked her about the significance of butterflies. She told me she became enthralled with butterflies during a vacation in Puerto Rico where she visited a butterfly museum. The storefront attached to the museum exclusively featured everything and anything to do with butterflies. Her experience compelled her to begin collecting butterflies on that trip, and she has been an avid collector ever since.

When I asked her if she had any knowledge of the butterfly symbolism as an afterlife communication, she replied she had only heard about it, but wasn't very informed.

So, I began telling her my limited knowledge and the four experiences and butterfly sightings I encountered during my father-in-law's passing.

After talking for a while, she confided that her father had bought her a Christmas gift, months before he died and upon his passing her mother gave it to her. She waited until Christmas to open it and to her surprise, it was a beautiful blanket filled with all different types of butterflies.

Her father hadn't bought anyone else in the family a present and it was unusual for him to have ordered something so far in advance for the holidays.

Replaying the scenario in her head she felt he must have known his end was near and knowing how much his daughter loved butterflies, he just had to buy this specific gift for her.

She became overwhelmed with emotion as she talked about the events, but also felt a sigh of relief believing he was truly still with her.

The blanket was kept on the back of her couch. Her husband and son were given strict instructions never to touch this blanket. A few months later, she was lying down on the couch and gently laid the blanket over herself. Without any explanation, the blanket began to tighten up around her as if her body was being shrink wrapped. This really startled her, and she never put the blanket over herself again. Partly out of fear it would happen again and partly out of fear that it wouldn't.

Her father's passing had been very difficult to accept, however her son's prophetic comments at key times never seemed to amaze her.

One day she was crying, and her six-year-old said, "Mommy, there are people who are bucket fillers and people who are bucket dippers. Bucket fillers fill people's buckets with love and dippers take love out of people's buckets. Because you're so sad, I filled your bucket with extra love this morning." When she questioned where he heard the story of the buckets, he couldn't tell her where he had heard it. He had no religious education and neither she nor her husband ever heard of the bucket fillers and dippers story.

He then went on to comfort his mother by explaining to her that grandpa was in heaven with his mommy and daddy, his family, and his favorite dog.

Her young son's telephone call to his grandfather seemed incredibly well timed and Kathy still questions his actions. What made him do it? Why was he so incredulous about speaking to his grandfather at that specific moment? Did he sense something that adults could not? Was the bucket story being delivered from God via her son? What's truly amazing is how a parent could find comfort in their child's innocent words.

2 Thessalonians 3:16

Now may the Lord of peace Himself give you peace at all times in all ways. The Lord be with all of you.

Chapter 10
Anger and Forgiveness

Ecclesiastes 7:9

Don't become angry quickly, because getting angry is foolish.

After a short period of time, our feelings of grief turned into sadness and eventually turned into anger.

How could that doctor that was treating my father-in-law for years have been so cavalier and disrespectful of my father-in-law's life?

An eye for an eye, and I wanted to punish him so he couldn't hurt anyone ever again.

Suing him, discrediting him, and ruining his life the way he ruined ours was constantly at the forefront of my mind.

Fortunately, my cousin, Christopher, is a malpractice attorney. So, I called him for advice and he explained we had a case, but that I should take some time to think about it.

Proverbs 14:29

Patient people have great understanding, but people with quick tempers show their foolishness.

The case could go on in the courts for years, and the family would need to be prepared to continue reliving this painful experience.

We'd eventually win the malpractice case, if we pursued legal action, and the courts would then determine what my father-in-law's life was financially worth. He was 82 years old, and retired with no dependents so what was the value of his life? These were horrible realities of suing the doctor who I felt killed my father-in-law.

After discussing it with Jody and her sisters, we decided to let it go and get on with our lives. There was no dollar amount that could replace the memories my father-in-law gave us. Love has no price!

My cousin gave me the best advice and the path to healing our sorrow and broken hearts.

Colossians 3:13

Get along with each other and forgive each other. If someone does wrong to you, forgive that person because the Lord forgave you.

Anger and forgiveness are two of the most difficult emotions to control. But following the loving teachings of Jesus Christ and accepting the Holy Spirit's inner guidance helps to free us from sorrow and pain.

Reading scripture helps to control these emotions and reinforces my decisions to just let it go.

I remind myself God has a plan that supersedes the emotions that are stirring up inside of me.

2 Corinthians 3:17

The Lord is the Spirit, and where the Spirit of the Lord is, there is freedom.

Chapter 11
Faith

It's easy to surrender your heart over to faith, but it's very difficult to intellectually surrender and accept faith as being reality.

There are those who don't share your same beliefs and even friends may feel you're out of touch and possibly even make jokes at your expense to try and show off their intellectual superiority. But those with faith understand the joke is on those who live without it.

Faith gets us through the most difficult and challenging times of our lives. And people with faith are not alone in this world because regardless of one's religious affiliation, believing in one God is universal and God represents faith.

Hebrews 11:3

It is by faith we understand that the whole world was made by God's command so what we see was made by something that cannot be seen.

Christians often say God is in you, and Christ is in you, or the Holy Spirit is in you.

This is a tough one to wrap your arms around. It's difficult to comprehend because how could three entities be one? This is my simplistic opinion … God is the essence of love; all that is good and the spiritual connection we have with others. Jesus Christ is called the Son of God, but he is God and came to us in human form because that's what our minds would allow us to accept. As a man, Christ instructed us on what it took to be a good person. He preached on forgiveness and taught us how to love one another. Jesus Christ provided us a fresh new start in life, a do-over. Or if you're a golfer, a spiritual mulligan.

To prove how much God loves us, He had to make a real big impression and one that would last forever. So, He allowed Himself as Jesus Christ to be brutally crucified. And God's existence is present in each of us through the Holy Spirit.

John 12:44-45

Then Jesus cried aloud: "Whoever believes in me believes not in me but in Him who sent me. And whoever sees me sees Him who sent me."

Jesus Christ and the Holy Spirit are one spiritual entity that guides us and tells us what's right from wrong, leads us down the right paths and provides us with wonderful daily opportunities to better ourselves. Faith gives us the ability to recognize God's messages and provides the courage to act upon those opportunities. Faith is an attribute that can change one's life for the better.

John 3:16

For God so loved the world that He gave His one and only Son, that whoever believes in Him shall not perish but have eternal life.

As I mature and get older, my five key senses of sight, sound, smell, taste, and touch are becoming dulled and not as keen as they once were. I marvel at how sharp and keen my grandchildren's key senses are. They play with my glasses and can see things I can't, the volume on my TV hurts their ears so they typically turn the volume down, they smell when the dog needs a bath way before I do, they're much more sensitive to hot and cold temperatures and constantly adjusting the thermostats, and they don't use as much salt and pepper as I do to season their food. I must admit, younger persons are much better in tune with their five key senses.

Psalm 51:10

Create in me a clean heart, O God, and put a new and right spirit within me.

I watch in marvel when my young, innocent grandchildren have complete conversations with their special invisible friends. It saddens me to know as they grow up those conversations will end, and they'll lose those comforting companions and special friends. I remember having my own special invisible friends when I was very young, but they also disappeared as I got older.

Parents and the other adults would typically observe youngsters talking to imaginary friends and chalk it up to a young kid's wild imagination. But is it their imaginations or is it their keen senses that enable them to detect what adults could no longer see, hear, touch, smell, or taste? Do young children have the unique ability to recognize spirits in another dimension or their guardian angels who may possibly be a loved one who had passed from this worldly life? We'll never know while we are still alive, but I find the thought interesting and one to consider.

My oldest grandson, Nicky, had a very interesting experience that I remember very well. The date was March 31st 2010, and the third anniversary of Sue's father's passing. Sue was getting dressed in her bedroom when she overheard her son Nicky, who was about 14 months old, talking to himself in the hallway. Then she noticed he wasn't talking to himself, but actually playing hide and seek in the opposite direction of where she was standing. Suzy watched in amazement as he played and interacted with an imaginary person, as he dodged behind one of the doorways. He was giggling and laughing at what seemed like the air. Nicky was totally oblivious to Suzy or anything else around him. His total attention was directed toward someone or something. Although he didn't speak comprehensible words, he was very excited and babbling out loud in the same way he would try to communicate with us. His dancing back and forth and playfulness toward nothing that could be seen or heard was mesmerizing.

At that precise moment, Sue began thinking about her father, his image appeared in her mind then she realized the significance of the date. It was March 31st the third anniversary of her father's passing.

My mother Irma told me of a similar experience she had as a young girl. She had a much older brother named Dario and he was a professional high diver. When he was 21 years old, he was performing a high dive act off the pier in Seaside Heights, NJ.

Something went wrong and as he hit the water, he broke his neck and died. According to my mother, as a young girl, Dario would come and speak to her. She vividly recalled Dario appearing and talking with her when she was alone. On several occasions her mother would hear her speaking to Dario, and she would get very upset and take my mother Irma to the cemetery where she would cry at her son's graveside.

Revelation 21:4

He will wipe every tear from their eyes. Death will be no more; mourning and crying and pain will be no more, for the first things have passed away.

My mother had another brother named Ronnie whom she was extremely close to. He was a wonderful person and my favorite uncle. He was a strong, good looking, athletic guy with wavy dark hair and he always had a unique twinkle in his eyes. My mother loved her protective big brother, and he would do anything for her.

I loved and respected him so much that I asked him to be my confirmation sponsor and chosen Godfather. Uncle Ronnie was so honored by my request he took me shopping and bought me a watch. I picked out one of those slip-on metal bands, but I was so skinny I had to settle on a leather band that we could add extra holes to so the watch would fit my wrist. I loved the watch, but really treasured the opportunity of shopping with my Uncle Ronnie.

Jeremiah 15:18

Why is my pain increasing, my wound incurable, refusing to be healed? Truly, you are to me like a deceitful brook, like waters that fall.

At age 52, he was diagnosed with lung cancer and his prognosis wasn't hopeful from the very start. My mother was devastated and had a very difficult time accepting the news.

I was working for Stetson Hat Company at the time Uncle Ronnie lost his dark, thick curly hair from the chemotherapy, so I brought him several styles of cowboy hats. I'd visit him as often as I could, and he tried hard to stay strong for everyone even while the side effects of his treatments made him terribly sick. He became a shell of his former self and had physically deteriorated, but that unique twinkle in his eye never dimmed.

Psalm 55:4-5

My heart is in anguish within me, the terrors of death have fallen upon me. Fear and trembling come upon me.

My mother was at the hospital waiting outside Ronnie's room when his wife, Lorraine, told her he was asking only for her. She went into his room alone and immediately saw the fear in his eyes. He was trying to tell her something but was unable to speak. He kept trying to motion with his eyes and head as my mother asked him questions. Finally, she asked, "Ronnie, do you see momma and dad?" He signaled yes by blinking his eyes and moving his head up and down. Ronnie was frightened and seemed to know what was about to happen.

My mother began to cry and calmly said, "It's OK Ron, they're here to take you with them. Don't be afraid to go with them Ronnie." Her words had a profound impact on his demeanor and my uncle immediately began to relax. A soothing look came upon his face and his eyes began to shine brightly. Just as he was about to take his last breath, my mother gave him the confirmation and comfort he needed. Her words were meaningful, and she held his hands as he surrendered and let himself go.

Thessalonians 3:16

Now, may the Lord of peace, Himself give you peace, at all times, in all ways. The Lord be with all of you.

My mother connected with both of her brothers because she believed and had faith. They knew she would understand and be able to accept what others couldn't see, hear, smell, touch, or taste.

Ronnie knew my mother's experience with Dario, and he needed her spiritual confirmation to let go and join his mother, father, and older brother Dario.

1 Peter 3:8-9

Although you have not seen Him, you love Him; and even though you do not see Him now, you believe in Him and rejoice with an indescribable and glorious joy, for you are receiving the outcome of your faith, the salvation of your souls.

My mother's faith provided her brother Ronnie the spiritual confirmation to surrender his fears and allow his mother and father to guide him to the other side. My mother's faith was a true gift from God.

There were three people my mother constantly talked about during her last days. Ronnie, her mother who she absolutely adored, and the man she met at age 13, married at 20 and loved for 71 of her 84 years, her husband and my father, Frank.

John 11:25-26

Jesus said to her, "I am the resurrection and the life. Those who believe in me, even though they die, will live, and everyone who lives and believes in me will never die. Do you believe this?"

Maybe we're all born with faith, and we can innocently connect with spirits during our younger years when our key senses are functioning at their highest and most sensitive levels. But as we grow older our senses slowly become dulled from all those extra mind deadening activities like TV, video games, loud noises, even soda, junk food, alcohol, and the real killer of our sense … stress.

Psalm 6:7

My eyes waste away because of grief. They grow weak because of all my foes.

As adults we have enormous responsibilities, like taking care of the family, performing well at work, making a good living and being a good provider, constantly worrying about what's going on in the world and how it's going to affect our lives. It's like a torturous 24/7 water drop treatment that before you know it deteriorates your senses and may make you a little negative, jaded and test your faith. When this happens, it's good to get a spiritual transfusion and reconnect with God. Remember God will give you faith and God is in you. Feel Christ in you and listen to the Holy Spirit within you.

This philosophy is beautifully summed up in **Psalm 62:1-2**

For God alone my soul waits in silence; from Him comes my salvation. He is my rock and my salvation, my fortress; I shall never be shaken.

Faith is believing in an afterlife and that your spirit will never die. I absolutely without any question or doubt know that this is true. I was blessed to have had many afterlife communications and interventions, starting with my father-in-law, and continuing with my father, mother, and in later years with my mother-in-law.

I'm sure I had many experiences with loved ones that had passed during my lifetime, but unfortunately my eyes, mind and heart weren't opened up yet to recognize those events as ADC signs and in many other instances, God's Divine Interventions. Like so many people who do not have unwavering faith, I viewed these prior events as pure coincidences. I am blessed to have been enlightened through afterlife connections with my father-in-law and parents and to have replaced believing in coincidences with unwavering faith.

James 1:6 Faith Beyond Doubt

But ask in faith, never doubting, for the one who doubts is like a wave of the sea, driven and tossed by the wind.

I also believe God, Christ and the Holy Spirit are in me and the essence of my soul, so my life is always being guided by God.

It's up to me to recognize what His plan is for me is and to foster up the courage to act on opportunities He puts before me.

1 Peter 1:8-9 Believing without seeing

Although you have not seen Him, you love Him; and even though you do not see Him now, you believe in Him and rejoice with an indescribable and glorious joy, for you are receiving the outcome of your faith, the salvation of your souls.

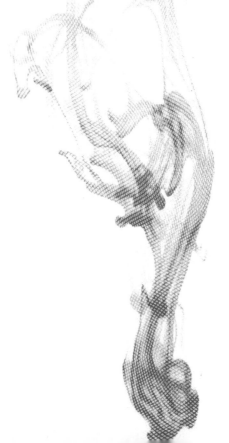

Chapter 12
Proof Positive

My daughter-in-law Sue was twenty-two weeks and four days into her second pregnancy when she was diagnosed with placenta previa, a pregnancy complication where the placenta grows at the lowest part of the womb and covers either part or all of the cervix.

On Christmas Day she began to hemorrhage, and Kris rushed her to the hospital. Fortunately, the bleeding stopped, and she was confined to bed rest for the duration of her pregnancy. All seemed well during Suzy's OBGYN examination on January 19th however, as the receptionist was scheduling her follow-up appointment she began to hemorrhage violently. The nurses called for an ambulance and within minutes she was admitted into the hospital, which luckily is located right across the street.

This can be a life-threatening condition for both the mother and baby and Sue was told she would most likely remain in the hospital for the duration of her pregnancy. She remained in bed for every minute of the next eleven days, but she still experienced various levels of bleeding.

Ecclesiastes 11:5

Just as you do not know how the breath comes to the bones in the mother's womb, so you do not know this work of God, who makes everything.

Then on Saturday January 30th, just before 3:00 AM, she began to hemorrhage, and this time the bleeding didn't stop. Within minutes she was crashing, and her blood pressure dropped to a critical 40 over 10. Her attending nurse called the life-saving team, Sue's doctor, the neonatal intensive care unit (NICU), and Kris. Everyone arrived in the operating room within a few minutes. Her doctor drove from his home to the hospital in a record breaking four minutes, and after dropping their first son, Nicholas off at our house, Kris sped to the hospital and went up the elevator to the operating room in the NICU.

Sue gave birth by emergency caesarian section to their second son, Joseph, at exactly 3:33 AM. As the doctors and nurses worked frantically to save Sue and their new baby, Kris called to tell me Sue gave birth to a boy. He even text a picture of his new son as the team of neonatal intensive care doctors and nurses began to work on him.

Nicholas was sleeping on my chest as I stared at the ceiling in our bedroom, feeling helpless and worrying about Sue and my new grandson.

Daniel 10:8-9

So, I was left alone to see this great vision. My strength left me, and my complexion grew deadly pale, and I retained no strength. Then I heard the sound of His words; and when I heard the sound of His words, I fell into a trance, face to the ground.

Somewhere between 4:00 AM and 4:30 AM my father-in-law ap-peared before me in a vision or apparition. I feel it was an appari-tion because I had never experienced any dream like this before. He looked just as he did before he passed, wearing his favorite gray sweatshirt and light tan khaki pants. He floated directly in front of me just a few feet away and spoke without moving his lips. The only thing he said was, "They're putting it in him." His image wasn't fright-ening, but his message was unsettling and confusing. I didn't un-derstand and asked, "What's in him?" My mind was swirling, did the doctors leave something inside Sue or the baby? What did he mean?

I asked him out loud, "What's in him?" He repeated "They're putting it in him." About 30 seconds went by and nothing more was said, and he just floated away into thin air and disappeared.

I didn't stop thinking about what my father-in-law said and I couldn't fall asleep until around 6:30 AM. The phone rang again at 7:30 AM and it was Sue assuring us she was OK and not to worry.

She said Kris was exhausted so she sent him home to get some rest and he'd be by soon to pickup Nicky. Sue told us she hadn't seen her new son yet and asked us to come to the hospital as soon as we could.

Jody and I went to the hospital later in the afternoon and imme-diately took Suzy to see her new 2 pound 6 ounce son for the first time.

As we entered Joey's private room in the Neo Intensive Care Unit, one of his neonatal doctors and dedicated nurses shifted their atten-tion directly to Joey's concerned mother and grandparents.

The doctor began to explain what was done and how hard they had to work on Joey. She said, "He really made us work hard, but we were able to get everything in him through his belly button and we also gave him a complete body blood transfusion and it was tough with his tiny veins, but we were able to get it in him quickly. He's small but we were able to intubate him, and we got the breathing tube in him."

They're putting it in him ... they're putting it in him ... my father-in-law's words kept ringing in my ears. Goose bumps ran up my spine and tears welled up in my eyes.

1 Kings 10:7

But I did not believe the reports until I came, and my own eyes had seen it. Not even half had been told me, Your wisdom and propriety, far surpass the report that I had heard.

We prayed every night the insurance company would allow Suzy to remain in the hospital. And our prayers where definitely answered. There is no doubt Suzy and baby Joey would never have survived if they hadn't been just feet away from the operating room and minutes from specialized doctors and nurses. Thank God for Sue's attending nurse whose experience and alertness saved Sue's life and gave her premature baby a fighting chance.

Their baby was baptized Joseph Fredrick Scelba on the second day of his life. As Jody and I drove home from the hospital I told her about her father coming to me in a vision and telling me "they're putting it in him." She began to cry and then asked me, "Did you see the exact time Joey was born?" I said, "Yes 3:33 AM" and she said, "That was the house number my father was born in, grew up in and lived in up to the time he went into the service."

It's interesting that **Jeremiah 33:3 says:**

Call to me and I will answer you and will tell you great and hidden things that you have not known.

Seeing Joey in the NICU of Morristown Memorial Hospital was my moment of enlightenment and the astonishing event that changed my life forever.

Habakkuk 1:5

Look at the nations and see! Be astonished! Be astounded! For a work is being done in your days that you would not believe if you were told.

My eyes were finally opened, and all my doubts were put to rest with Joey's birth.

Through my father-in-law, God sent me a message and it was as if He was asking me directly, "Do you get it now?" And I most definitely did!

The events surrounding Joey's birth changed my way of thinking and how I view things. The experience opened my mind up to accepting unlimited possibilities that can't be identified with my five key senses. God's message changed my perspectives, values, and the way I treat my fellow man. It was the turning point that instilled my unwavering faith, spiritual enrichment, and my belief that God and the afterlife do exist.

Job 28:20

"Where then does wisdom come from? And where is the place of understanding?"

I believe these events were truly Divine Interventions delivered to me through my father-in-law. It was the turning point when I intellectually and emotionally accepted my spiritual journey and newly found beliefs. My views, opinions and overall life significantly changed.

While these events are very personal, I'm not embarrassed to share them with anyone who is struggling with their own faith and belief in God. Faith can be challenging and maybe sharing my story is part of God's overall plan for me. These miraculous events influenced my spiritual calling and inspired me to create my own personal layman ministry.

2 Peter 1:10

Therefore, brothers and sisters be all the more eager to confirm your call and election, for if you do this, you will never stumble.

I have no doubt God sent my father-in-law to be Joey's Guardian Angel, and once again he gave me what I desired most … confirmation and proof positive that God does exist, and the afterlife is real.

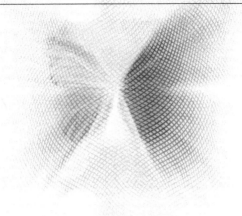

Chapter 13
Life's Greatest Miracle

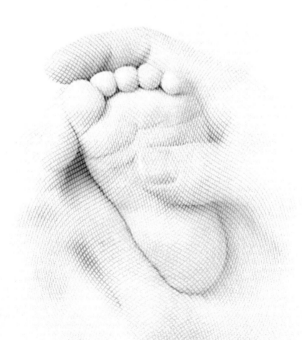

Ecclesiastes 11:5

Just as you do not know how the breath comes to the bones in the mother's womb, so you do not know the work of God, who makes everything.

People often say birth is a miracle and it's a true blessing from God.

Our family is extremely blessed with six healthy, happy, beautiful grandchildren. The births of Nicky, Sofia, Gia, Sienna, and Mikey were miracles and blessings from God. But Joey's birth was an extra special miracle. He was a blessing that truly gave me a newfound relationship and connection with God and instilled an unwavering faith in my soul that nothing could ever change.

Joey was born when Sue was in her 26th week so his gestation was at only six and a half months. He decided to be born 10 weeks earlier than his expected date, so Joey had to spend three and a half months in a very special NICU at Morristown Memorial Hospital.

I believe God has a special plan for each of my grandchildren, but I'm sure He has an extra special plan for Joey because he fought so hard to get healthy and is one strong guy who faced all types of life-threatening challenges head on and beat all the odds.

When Joey was in the hospital, the deadly MRSA virus spread throughout his NICU and almost all the babies contracted the infection. Many became very sick and sadly died.

Joey also became infected with the virus, but he was determined to fight and had a strong will to live and was one of only 25% of the NICU babies that beat the infection.

Joshua 1:5

No one shall be able to stand against you all the days of your life. As I was with Moses, so I will be with you; I will not fail you or forsake you.

Joey was never alone in the NICU, and we all visited with him every single day for the entire time he was in the hospital. He finally came home during Mother's Day weekend. This was a wonderful surprise and the best Mother's Day gift Sue could have received.

All our friends and family came to see and meet cute, little, fighter Joey and they were all amazed at how tough he was. Yes, Joey was an extraordinary miracle and the ultimate blessing from God. But after only two days Joey started having trouble breathing, so in the middle of the night Suzy rushed him back to the hospital.

Romans 12:12

Rejoice in hope, be patient in suffering, preserve in prayer.

As Sue raced into the emergency room with Joey, the nurses immediately recognized his condition and realized he was in distress. They grabbed him from Sue and immediately began administering life-saving CPR measures.

Sue sat all alone in an empty hallway as the doctors and nurses once again worked to save Joey's life. Suzy had her eyes closed and was praying when suddenly she heard a woman's voice say, "he'll be OK."

Sitting next to her was a strange woman in her fifties with brown hair that she hadn't noticed before and it was as if she appeared out of thin air. Sue hadn't seen nor spoken to this woman, and she just appeared out of nowhere. Sue was praying and crying, but this stranger said the exact right thing at exactly the right moment. "Don't worry, he'll be OK." Sue just nodded and when she closed her eyes the woman was gone. She vanished into thin air and disappeared, just as strangely as she appeared.

Hebrews 2:10

It was fitting that God for whom and through whom all things exist, in bringing many children to glory, should make the pioneers of their salvation perfect through sufferings.

Joey was re-admitted into the hospital and spent another month getting his little lungs healthier and stronger.

Sixth Butterfly Sighting

Before going to her daily visit with Joey in the NICU, Suzy got Nicholas ready for daycare. After dropping Nicky off, Suzy stopped at a Dunkin Donuts for a cup of coffee. She put the radio on after getting back in the car and was surprised to find the radio on an AM station that she never listens to playing one of her father Fred's favorite songs. Sue couldn't understand how the radio changed from FM to AM and why it was programmed to that specific oldie station.

As Sue walked into the NICU room to see Joey she was greeted by a new nurse she had never seen or met before.

She introduced herself and as the nurse was explaining how Joey was doing Sue became mesmerized by what the nurse was wearing. From head to toe her scrubs were covered in butterflies.

A sixth butterfly sighting and another message from her father Fred.

The radio station and the butterflies on the nurse's scrubs just might have been Fred connecting in his own personal way to comfort and tell Suzy everything will be OK.

After spending another six weeks in the hospital, Joey finally came home. Everyone felt he was truly a miracle baby and destined to do great things in this world. God gave Joey the strength and endurance to survive his greatest challenges for a specific purpose.

Isaiah 40:29-31

He gives power to the faint and strengthen the powerless. Even youths will faint and be weary, and the young will fall exhausted; but those who wait for the Lord shall renew their strength, they shall mount up with wings like eagles, they shall run not be weary, they shall walk and not faint.

I'm sure at some point in the future Joey will recognize the unique connection he has with God.

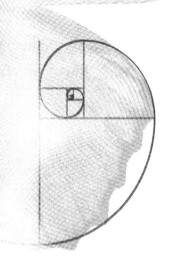

Chapter 14
My Father's Confirmations

Psalm 20:7

The righteous walk in integrity – happy are the children who follow them!

A few years before my father Frank's passing, we attended a concert performed by the New Jersey Symphony. This was always an extra special event because when the symphony was first established, my father was the principal flutist for the symphony and a featured soloist in the orchestra. So naturally these concerts brought back wonderful memories for both my father and mother. My father was also the major influence in my musical background.

We were sitting in one of those premium boxes reserved for VIP guests and I was looking out at the stage. In my head, I was counting the number of musicians, stage lights and sound speakers. This was something I did at literally every concert I attended regardless of the genre. It became a habit that I couldn't help myself from doing. I'd count, then recount and recount over and over just to make sure I had the correct numbers. It really was an uncontrollable compulsion.

I remember my father looking at me with puzzlement and then he finally asked me what I was doing. I sheepishly told him I was counting and that I can't help myself. Wherever I go I count all type of things, people, lights, tile blocks, pictures on the wall ... everything. Every time I go to a concert, I count the number of musicians, lights, and speakers.

Then, he said, "I never knew you were a counter, so am I." He told me wherever he went he also couldn't help himself from counting all types of objects like ceiling blocks and lights. When he went to a concert, he'd also count the musicians, speakers, risers, and lights just like me.

We lived our entire lives and never knew we both had this peculiar counting habit. I remember feeling better and reassured knowing I wasn't alone, that he had this same weird compulsion and that I wasn't nuts.

This ended up being one of those unique connections my father and I had with one another. We were both counters and no one else knew our little strange secret.

Another interesting connection we had with numbers was our birthdays. My father's birthday is 7-11 and my birthday is 11-7 and these are two Psalms with those same numbers, and both speak to God's righteousness.

Psalm 7:11

God is a righteous judge, and a God who has indignation every day.

Psalm 11:7

For the Lord is righteous; He loves righteous deeds; the upright shall behold His face.

Our personal numbers were 11 and 7, but it wasn't until moments after his passing that I realized the spiritual significance 11 and 7 had in our relationship.

My father Frank was in his forties when he developed angina, a heart condition. He underwent quadruple bypass surgery at age 63 and suffered his first heart attack just a few weeks following the procedure. After experiencing a series of additional heart attacks, he had multiple stents implanted, and then required another triple bypass surgery at age 76. He finally died in my arms when his heart literally couldn't find another beat. He passed from conjunctive coronary disease at age 87 on November 20, 2015, at 1:13 AM, but the official recorded time of death was 1:17 AM. He loved his family, loved his friends, loved life, and was a determined fighter who did everything the doctors told him to do to stay alive.

James 5:16

Therefore, confess your sins to one another, and pray for one another, so that you may be healed. The prayer of the righteous is powerful and effective.

I was with him when his cardiologist gave him the sad news that there was nothing more they can do to keep him alive. With great compassion, he told my father he should go home and spend his last loving times with his family.

Knowing the end was near, my father made a special effort to talk to each of us alone. We had our disagreements and ups and downs over the years, but we always had a strong relationship and were always there for one another, so it was easy to make amends with some old misunderstandings.

Mark 4:11-12

And He said to them, "To you has been given the secret of the Kingdom of God, but for those outside, everything comes in parables; in order that they may indeed look, but not perceive, and may indeed listen, but not understand; so that they may not turn again and be forgiven."

My father was a self-proclaimed agnostic, which I feel was attributed to his earlier parochial school experiences. It wasn't unusual in those days for the new Italian immigrants to be openly discriminated against by the earlier Irish immigrants.

Unfortunately for my father, the parochial school he attended was run by an order of Irish priests and nuns. To make things worse, he was left-handed and the church unknowingly thought left-handed dominance was a trait of the devil. I can only imagine what this little dark, left-handed Sicilian boy had to endure.

James 2:1-4

My brothers and sisters, do you with your acts of favoritism really believe in our glorious Lord Jesus Christ? For if a person with gold rings and in fine clothes comes into your assembly, and if a poor person in dirty clothes also comes in, and if you take notice of the one wearing the fine clothes and say, "Have a seat here, please," while to the one who is poor you say, "Stand over there," or "Sit at my feet," have you not made distinctions among yourselves, and become judges with evil thoughts?

Being an agnostic didn't mean he didn't believe in God or an afterlife. It just meant he was honest and wasn't embarrassed to admit he didn't know.

Shortly before he died, we spoke at great length about faith and the afterlife. I have no doubt he was a true believer in a higher power and an afterlife. He told me he was confident death was not the end, but the beginning of something greater. My father believed his soul or spirit could possibly be converted into some sort of electric energy or force and be transferred into another spiritual dimension.

John 6:46-47

No one has seen the Father except the One who is from God; only He has seen the Father. I tell you the truth, whoever believes has eternal life.

Toward his final days we'd discuss family issues, complexities of the world and more.

He'd end almost every discussion with the words … "It is, what it is." At the time, I didn't appreciate how thoughtful and insightful his five simple words were. And it wasn't until two years after his death when I was thinking about him that I put two and two together and realized he was actually reciting his own version of the Serenity Prayer.

Being a man who got straight to the point, my father edited the short version of The Serenity Prayer from 27 words down to his own simple but powerful, profound version for acceptance and surrender … "It is, what it is."

Colossians 3:8

But now also put things out of your life: anger, bad temper, doing or saying things to hurt others, and using evil words when you talk.

His five insightful words were comforting and a gift because they brought me back to my favorite 27 profound words that changed my life … The Serenity Prayer. All was good, and I felt a sense of relief and experienced immediate peace with the situation. My father lived by the golden rule, but also had his own personal edited interpretation of The Serenity Prayer. His parting advice for surrender and acceptance … "It is, what it is."

Psalm 23

The Lord is my Shepard I shall not want He makes me lie down in green pastures and leads me beside still waters. He restores my soul and takes me down the righteous path for His name sake. And even though I may travel in the valley of darkness I shall fear no evil Your rod and staff protect me. You prepare a table for me before my enemies, You anoint my head in oil and my cup over-flows and surely goodness and mercy shall follow me all the days of my life, for I shall dwell in the house of the Lord for all my days long.

The room was quiet, the lights were dim, and I sat on the side of his bed. Holding his hand in my left hand while cradling and supporting his head with my right I spoke in a soft comforting voice. "I'm right here, I'll never leave your side, you are a great man. You've done an exceptional job, nothing to worry about. It's OK to go, I promise we'll take care of Mom. You'll be with your father and mother and everyone that loves you. If there is any way possible to contact me please try, or just give me a sign that there is an afterlife."

These were the last words I kept repeating as I fought back my tears. Never taking my eyes off his face and the pulsing artery on the right side of his neck. I watched as my father closed his eyes and took his very last breath at exactly 1:13 AM on November 20, 2015.

When the nurse came into the room, I told her the exact time of death was 1:13 AM. She acknowledged my comment and proceeded to check his heartbeat with her stethoscope. She turned, looked up at the clock on the wall and said official time of death is 1:17AM. I told her, "Well, that's not really the official time of death, he took his last breath and his heart stopped pumping at exactly 1:13." She just looked at me and said, "I know, but the official time of death is 1:17."

It bothered me that she was going to record the wrong time of death, but then again what difference did it really make? My father just died and now I had to make the calls to my family and figure out what to do next.

I sent my brother a text because I knew he was sleeping and would be up in just a few hours. Next I called my sister and brother-in-law to break the news and we agreed it would be better to tell my mother in person first thing in the morning.

It was hard to witness my father's health deteriorating so quickly and the last couple of weeks were especially difficult to emotionally handle. He was in the hospital for weeks, then transferred to a palliative care facility where he finally passed. We all took shifts being by his side. My brother had the early morning, my mother stayed all day, my sister took the early evening and I put him to bed each night.

My father's entire family, including his six great grandchildren, visited Pop-Pop Frank every chance we had, and his room was always buzzing with people coming and going.

2 Timothy 4:16-17

At my first defense no one came to my support, but all deserted me. May it not be counted against them! But the Lord stood by me and gave me strength so that through me the message might be fully proclaimed, and all the Gentiles might hear it.

I was alone with my father's body, collecting his things and cleaning up his room before driving home in the middle of the night.

A very nice aide helped me carry his belongings down to my car and said beautiful things about my father. Even in the short time he was there, he and my mother managed to make friends with the entire staff.

I thanked him for helping me and his kind words and then got into my SUV and started my 20 minute drive home.

As I drove north on Route 287, the nurse's call of his official time of death at 1:17 kept popping into my head and I started talking to myself. "What was the big deal? Why couldn't she have recorded the correct time … he didn't die at 1:17 he died at exactly 1:13." It really bothered me that she recorded the wrong time of death … 1:17, 1:17 why 117 …117? Then it hit me … my birthday is 11-7, and if that wasn't strange enough, my father's birthday is 7-11.

As I continued to drive home, my tears of sadness and sorrow immediately turned into tears of joy and happiness. As my father took his final breaths, I asked him to please give me a sign if there is an afterlife and he gave me a resounding confirmation that there is without question or doubt, life after this world and I am right to believe.

To better understand the significance of these two numbers I did a little biblical research on the numbers 11 and 7.

Eleven has great significance in the bible and considered a master number. It is used 24 times and "11th" is counted at an additional 19 times. It is associated with faith and psychics and viewed as a dynamic, charismatic and the most intuitive and instinctive of all numbers. However, 11 also represents disorder, judgement, and chaos, the direct opposite of the number 10, which represents law and order.

The gospel of John records eleven very special promises.

John 3:16

For God so loved the world that He gave His one and only son, that whoever believes in Him shall not perish but have eternal life.

John 6:54

Whoever eats my flesh and drinks my blood has eternal life, and I will raise them up on the last day.

John 8:12

When Jesus spoke again to the people, He said "I am the light of the world. Whoever follows me will never walk in darkness but will have the light of life."

John 8:31–32

To the Jews that believed Him, Jesus said, "if you hold to my teaching, you are really my disciples. Then you will know the truth, and the truth will set you free."

John 8:36

So if the Son sets you free, you will be free indeed.

John 12:26

Whoever serves me must follow me; and where I am, my servant also will be. My Father will honor the one who serves me.

John 14:12

I tell you the truth, anyone who has faith in me will do what I have been doing. He will do even greater things than these because I am going to the Father.

John 14:15–16

If you love me, you will obey what I command. And I will ask the Father, and He will give you another advocate, to be with you forever.

John 14:21

Whoever has my commands and obeys them, he is the one who loves me. He who loves me will be loved by my Father, and I too will love him and show myself to him.

John 15:5

I am the vine; you are the branches. If a man remains in me and I in him, he will bear much fruit; apart from me you can do nothing.

John 15:14

You are my friends if you do what I command.

Other references to the number 11:

Jesus Christ: Jesus is Lord; Our Redeemer; Savior Jesus; God in Heaven; and God Almighty all consist of 11 letters.

11 disciples remained after Judas hanged himself.

Many biblical scholars and theologians believe the number 11 represents the prophecy of the end of time, the 11th hour before the rapture and Armageddon when disorder and confusion will consume the world, as written in the Book of Revelation.

Isaiah 11:11

And it shall come to pass in that day, that the Lord shall set His hand again the second time to recover the remnant of His people, which shall be left, from Assyria, and from Egypt, and from Pathros, and from Cush, and from Elam, and from Shinar, and from Hamath, and from the islands of the sea.

Ezekiel 11:11

This city shall not be your pot, and you shall not be the meat inside it; I will judge you at the border of Israel.

Daniel 11:11

Moved with rage, the king of the south shall go out and do battle against the king of the north, who shall muster a great multitude, which shall, however, be defeated by his enemy.

Revelation 11:11

And after three days and a half the Spirit of life from God entered them, and they stood upon their feet; and great fear fell upon them which saw them.

Seven is considered the most significant of all the numbers in the bible and represents God's total spiritual perfection, completeness, and tonality.

God created the earth in six days and rested on the seventh, which is symbolic of total perfection and completeness.

The Book of Revelation speaks to seven bowls of wrath; seven seals; seven churches; seven trumpets: and seven spirits.

God's perfect judgment of everyone on earth, including those who do not recognize Jesus Christ as their Lord and Savior.

The Tribulation is also thought to have lasted for seven years.

I felt a much deeper connection with my father and a sense of peace and tranquility after learning the powerful biblical significance of the numbers 11 and 7.

Mark 9:23-24

Jesus said to him, "If you are able! All things can be done for the one who believes." Immediately the father of the child cried out, "I believe, help my unbelief!"

When I got home, Jody was waiting for me and we spoke for an hour or so about the events of the evening, my feelings and what the future may have in store for our family.

It was a little past 4:00 AM when I began to write my father's obituary notice on my computer. Suddenly, I received an e-mail alert … Bing, Bing … then seconds later another e-mail alert. I switched out of the word document I was working on and checked the e-mails.

Ten months earlier Jody and I had booked two non-refundable airline tickets to Austin, Texas to attend one of our closest friends, Mike and Carol Critchley's, son's wedding. But as my father's condition worsened, we couldn't leave him or our family at that critical time.

John 8:47

"Whomever is from God hears the words of God. The reason you do not hear them is that you are not from God."

I called the airline to cancel our tickets and asked about a refund or future credit. And anyone who has ever tried to get a refund for non-refundable airline tickets understands how difficult and frustrating the experience can be.

I spoke to a representative who explained to me the airline's policy and that I'd have to use the tickets before May and would also incur an additional $400 charge to change the tickets.

I couldn't believe the lack of sensitivity or compassion and was angry with the representative, so I told her exactly how I felt. She told me I could go online and try to request a refund but was pretty sure I'd be denied. Well, I searched for the right page and form to make my request and after two days, received a follow-up e-mail requesting a doctor's note or death certificate. I felt ridiculous asking the doctor for a note, but a few days before my father passed, she gave me a note and I forwarded it to the airline. I had already written off the money for the tickets and honestly didn't care.

Watching my father battle for his life, as well as the incredible stress and emotional anguish the family was going through made this situation completely insignificant.

To my surprise, both e-mails were from United Airlines notifying me they were happy to issue a total 100% refund for our two non-refundable tickets.

The chain of events surrounding the refund of our airline tickets meant something. It was the second sign and ADC confirming an afterlife that I received from my father just hours after his passing.

2 Timothy 1:14

Guard the good treasure entrusted to you, with the help of the Holy Spirit living in us.

The third peculiar incidence occurred the day of my father's wake at the funeral home. My father and I both owned the exact same gold necklace designed with alternating solid bars and thick woven rope chain. I added a plain gold cross and decorative gold coin to the necklace that my father-in-law Al always wore. I can't remember a day that he didn't wear that gold coin around his neck, and it had tremendous sentiment to me. Jody and her sisters gave me his gold coin, so I would always have something of my father-in-law's close to my heart.

Just as I had done a thousand times before, I unhooked the chain, held both ends straight out, stretching the chain so it wouldn't tangle and carefully laid it on top of my dresser.

After I showered, I took both ends and as I began to hold the chain up to attach it around my neck, the chain separated and split exactly in half. Not at the point where the bars met the rope, but directly in the middle of the thickest part of the rope chain.

This was another very weird event and once again I couldn't help but to think this was an intervention with a specific message that although we are now physically separated, he will always still be with me. My father was fulfilling my request by contacting me and confirming God's existence and that there was, in fact, an afterlife. I also interpreted this event with a deeper more meaningful message. Although, we were now physically separated, we will never be spiritually apart. The bonds we experience in this physical world have no hold over the spiritual connections we have forever.

Psalm 37:4

Take delight in the Lord, and He will give you the desires of your heart.

My father knew my need and deep desire to know. He came to me and gave me another precious gift of confirmation and proof, that God exists and not to fear … there really is an afterlife.

Chapter 15
Random Numbers

After my father's passing and our unique numerology connections, I felt compelled to research other biblical numerology references. I also began to explore other numerology correlations in my everyday life.

Psalm 104:15

And wine to gladden the human heart, oil to make the face shine, and bread to strengthen the human heart.

My first unexplainable numerology experience occured while I was making wine with a group of friends in September 2008, about one month following the passing of my father-in-law.

The facilty where we made wine had accumulated hundreds of barrels over the years. To keep things organized, each barrel was stenciled with the group's leader's name and an assigned barrel number. The stenciled barrel numbers were prominently displayed in a climate controlled warehouse of racks.

For some unknown reason, my barrel had my name stenciled on it, but the barrel was never assigned a number. When I notified the wine company's managers, they reviewed the 2007 records and assigned me number 7-13-07.

The numbers 7 and 13 just happen to be my lucky numbers. I was born on November 7th, my son's high school football jersey was number 7, my wife and I have 13 diamonds in our wedding rings, we flew out on our honeymoon on Friday the 13th, and our first grandson Nicky, was also born on the 7th. Over the years, the numbers 7 and 13 always seemed to come up in our favor.

A warm and comfortable feeling came over me when I saw this number now stenciled on my 2007 wine barrel.

We had a lot of fun making wine, so I invited a few other friends to join us for the 2008 crushing. I purchased another barrel and once again the barrel needed to be assigned a number registered to me.

I stood over the manager's shoulder as she glazed over a numbered sheet of paper that listed somewhere around fifty unassigned barrel numbers in sequential order. She moved her pencil down then up and then down the page again. About halfway down the page and in the middle of the list she stopped and said, "Why don't you take this one, number 08-18-08."

It seemed odd and didn't make sense for her not to assign me the first number at the top of the blank page and I remember thinking her actions were a bit strange.

It wasn't until my son Kris and I were driving home that I realized the significance of the number she chose for me, 08-18-08.

August 18, 2008, (08-18-08) was the date my father-in-law died in our arms, and I couldn't help but to swell up with emotion.

I believe the wine manager's actions weren't coincidences, but signs, interventions, or numerology communications from my father-in-law to reinforce my belief in God and the afterlife.

Another strange numbers event happened when I was going through paperwork while managing my father-in-law's estate. I had months of bank statements piled up on my desk and sticking out smack in the middle of the pile was the bottom of one online statement from Bank of America. The date printed on the bottom margin of the statement was 8/18/2008, again the date he died.

We had such a close relationship, and he knew I had a desperate desire to believe. I absolutely feel my father-in-law gave me ADC messages and because of our love, he gave me the ultimate gift to believe.

My father-in-law shared with me the meaning of wisdom and was guiding me through my journey to discover faith.

I'm not a numerologist, and never studied numerology, but this number thing was bizarre. So, I did a little research and learned some very interesting findings regarding numerology and the bible.

Numerology is found and referenced all throughout the Old and New Testaments. Some biblical scholars believe the placement and meanings of these numbers in scripture are messages from God and do not relate to simply numbers or quantities. Their spiritual interpretations represent qualities, values, and attributes. Not all theologians share or accept this belief and feel numbers simply relate to quantities.

But if you believe as I do, that there are no such things as coincidences, you'll be more inclined to believe in numerical symbolism.

I've explained the connection my father and I have with 7 and 11 and explained the biblical significance.

We both also enjoyed going to Las Vegas but neither of us ever gambled. But if we had, our 7 and 11would've certainly been winning numbers at the dice table.

Additional numerical references interpreted by biblical scholars can be found in the appendix of this book. Those numbers include: 3; 4; 6; 8; 9; 10; 12; 13; 40; 50; and 70.

Chapter 16
My Mother's Interventions

Proverbs 31:28-29

Her children rise up and call her happy; her husband too, and he praises her, "Many women have done excellently, but you surpass them all."

My mother died on June 25, 2018, one day before her 64th wedding anniversary and two years, six months after my father's death.

She missed my father terribly and truly died of a broken heart. My mother passed in the comforting arms of my sister, Carol, her husband, John, and myself. As we held her close, we repeatedly told her how much we loved her, that she was the absolute best mother, grandmother, and great-grandmother in the world and that it was OK to surrender herself and rejoin Dad.

She had told us for days that my father was in the room and that she was wearing a blue dress and they were dancing to "Tenderly," their wedding song.

Genesis 9:13

I have set my bow in the clouds, and it shall be a sign of the covenant between me and the earth.

When she died, it was a beautiful clear day and the sun was shining as we walked through the parking lot to our cars. Just as I got in my car, the skies turned black and opened up to a torrential downfall of rain. It only lasted for a few minutes, but it produced the most colorful, beautiful rainbow I had ever seen!!!

John 1:4

In Him was life, and the life was the light of all people.

My mother's formula for connecting with God was her deep belief in lighting church candles. She would light them while praying for family and friends who may be ill, suffering a loss, looking for a new job, or facing any type of challenge. Lighting church candles was her personal formula for connecting with God. After my father passed, I'd take her to the local Catholic parish so she could light candles and continue to make her special spiritual connection.

Psalm 119:105

Your word is a lamp to my feet and a light to my path.

I never walk barefoot or just in socks. I always wear shoes, sneakers, or slippers but when I arrived home, I was walking around the house aimlessly just in my socks. As I walked through the dining room, I stepped on a sharp object. I looked down and stuck to my sock was an old pink and white pre-lit birthday candle. This was certainly an odd situation because we hadn't celebrated a birthday in over a month and our cleaning people had just thoroughly vacuumed our dining room where I stepped on the candle.

But that was just the beginning of a series of peculiar events to occur. Right before we left for her one day viewing, I went to put on my repaired gold necklace with the attached gold cross and my father-in-law's gold coin. As I picked the chain up to put it on, the rope with the thick bars separated again in the exact same spot as it did on the day of my father's funeral viewing. Once again, a very strong sign or intervention with a specific ADC message telling me that although we were now physically separated, that she was with my father and father-in-law, and they would always be with me.

I felt her messages were coming through loud and clear. But there was more to come.

While I was standing in front of her casket, my good friend Tim approached me to pay his respects. I hadn't seen Timmy and his wife Terri since my father's funeral, only because he moved to Pennsylvania and we both had hectic work schedules. But we always had a good time when we got together, and I truly appreciated him driving the 70 plus miles from Pennsylvania to pay his respects.

As he put his hand out to mine, he placed a wrinkled card in my hand and said, "I wasn't sure I should give this to you, but Mike (a good mutual friend) told me it would be OK, and you'd understand." I opened my hand up and it was a dirty, wrinkled prayer card from my father's funeral two and a half years before.

Timmy is a fanatic about keeping a clean and orderly garage and he told me as he was getting into his car, he spotted something odd on his garage floor. He had his car professionally cleaned and detailed a few days before and being a neat freak, he swept his garage clean and couldn't understand how anything could've been on the floor. When he picked it up, it was my father's prayer card from the viewing he attended two and a half years before, with the Serenity Prayer printed on one side.

Deuteronomy 4:9

But take care and watch yourselves closely, so as neither to forget the things that your eyes have seen nor to let slip from your mind all the days of your life; make them known to your children and your children's children.

My mother was certainly coming through and confirming to me that the afterlife was real and most definitely exists.

But there were more signs, interventions, and confirmations yet to come. My mother let me know she was always there to help me, guide me and support me. It was a great comfort knowing I would never be alone.

It was September 17, 2019, one year and about three months after my mother had passed.

I was ready to retire and exit from my company of 36 years. I prepared all the documentation and planned on signing to execute my succession plan that evening.

The timing was right, and I truly felt God was directing my decision. But I still had some concerns, trepidations, and I was a bit reluctant to officially sign the final paperwork and walk away.

Seventh Butterfly Sighting

I kissed Jody goodbye and walked through the garage to my SUV parked in the driveway. As the garage door opened, I saw the most magnificent and majestic red, black, and orange Monarch butterfly just sitting on the side of my white SUV door. I instinctively put my left hand out and this beautiful creature flew directly onto my finger. I stumbled to get my phone out of my pocket with my right hand and quickly snapped a few pictures of this incredible event. I also wanted proof of this historical experience.

I said, "Thank you, Mom. I really needed a sign that I'm making the right decision and doing the right thing. I love you, continue to make yourself known and please guide me through these life-changing events."

It was as if the weight of the world was immediately lifted off my shoulders. I felt an amazing sigh of relief and we signed the succession documentation that night.

The following day I attended an awards reception for Megan, who a year earlier had become the first woman partner with 3E Public Relations, a PR firm I founded. Megan joined Patrick, who was my first hire over 30 years before, and longtime PR partner, to execute the succession plan of my public relations company.

The affair was held at a facility that housed a Top Golf simulator bar and grill, several dining restaurants, as well as an indoor mall of board-walk type games and booths. Nancy, a friend, marketing associate, and wonderful media outreach specialist, and I were wandering around the mall and came upon one of those water pistol balloon games. But instead of shooting water from a pistol into a clown's mouth, this one featured bathroom faucet fixtures that shot water into a toilet bowl that had a balloon attached to blow up.

Both being competitive, we bet on who'd win. I just barely beat her out by blowing up my balloon first.

Having six grandchildren means I need to bring six prizes home, and frankly I didn't see anything of interest, so I told Nancy to pick something out for herself.

Eighth Butterfly Sighting

Nancy said, "Why don't you choose one of those beautiful stuffed but-terflies?" I never even noticed the large colorful butterflies, but as soon as Nancy pointed them out, I chose the green, purple, pink and white one.

I didn't give it to anyone, because I felt my mother's presence again and I still keep that silly stuffed butterfly in my home office. It's a daily remind-er my mother is always guiding and protecting me and my family.

I am now very astute and witness the presence of butterflies everywhere I go. I see them on the golf course, my yard, the beach, the boat, and on walks and bike trails in Florida and New Jersey.

I'm convinced my mother, father, father-in-law, and mother-in-law are all watching over me and our family no matter where we are.

My mother Irma lived in love, and she lived in God and God lived in her.

1 Thessalonians 3:12

And may the Lord make you increase and abound in love for one another and for all just as we abound in love for you.

When people say God is in you, Christ is in you or the Holy Spirit is in you, that simply means love and all its virtues are in you, and my mother was simply pure love.

I have no doubt God's love lived in her, and she wasn't shy or embarrassed to share and spread God's special love with everyone she met.

1 Corinthians 14:1

Pursue love, and strive for spiritual gifts, and especially that you may prophesy.

My mother had the unique ability to make everyone feel extra special. And her talent expanded to being able to simultaneously participate in 20 different conversations and somehow make each person feel like they were the center of all her attention. She greeted every person with a wide-eyed expression of sincere happiness and welcomed them with only her irreplaceable words of, "Oh my God, how are you, my love?"

She was the most devoted daughter, sister, aunt, cousin, friend and the best, most loving wife, mother, mother-in-law, grandmother, and great-grandmother. There was no one that she didn't touch in an incredibly moving, inspirational, and positive way.

1 Corinthians 10:24

Do not seek your own advantage, but that of the other.

Sometimes we don't recognize or appreciate the impact our family members make on a society until they are gone. And that's normal because they're our fathers, mothers, brothers, and sisters ... so we may not really see how special they are or the significant role they play in other people's lives. Since my mother's passing, I've received literally hundreds of e-mails, text messages and phone calls from people all over the country. Cousins I haven't spoken to in 20 years, high school friends I haven't seen or spoken to in nearly 50 years, and many others all had the same beautiful comments and loving messages. "Dave, you have no idea how your mother helped and comforted me when I needed it the most. She was there for me without question or judgement. I loved her and miss her."

My mother gave of herself, and she gave out of the goodness of her heart. She was truly unselfish and deeply appreciated the thoughtfulness and caring touch of others. She had the uncanny ability to make everyone feel like they were the most important person in the world. From all the students she taught, to all her family and friends, to people who worked on her house and especially all the waiters and waitresses, who became independently wealthy because of her extremely generous tipping philosophy.

Even in her last days, she found the incredible strength, courtesy, respect, and love to acknowledge, thank, and compliment everyone who was helping her at the Care One facility where she peacefully and respectfully passed.

It's as if Apostle Paul wrote **Corinthians 13:1-8** about her:

If I speak in tongues of men and of angels, but have not love, I am only a resounding gong or clanging cymbal. If I have the gift of prophesy and can fathom all mysteries and knowledge and if I have faith that can move mountains, but have not love, I am nothing.

If I give all I possess to the poor and surrender my body to the flames but have not love, I gain nothing. Love is patient, love is kind. It does not envy, it does not boast, it is not proud. It is not rude, it is not self-seeking, it is not easily angered … it keeps no record of the wrongs. Love does not delight in evil but rejoices

with the truth. It always protects, always trusts, always hopes ... always perseveres. Love never fails.

People talk about walking toward the light. Well, my mother's essence lit up a room just like the thousands of candles she lit for so many of us during her lifetime.

We all have our own special memories of my mother Irma, and we can share the universal connection with the symbolism of the candle representing the light of her love.

Her light will forever burn brightly in our hearts, minds, and souls.

Chapter 17
God Will Provide

There's an old joke about a man who claimed to have total faith and that no matter what happened, God would provide for him.

It was the spring and heavy rains started pouring down. It rained so hard the streets began to flood. The police and National Guard drove up and down the streets in big four-wheel drive trucks rescuing people from their homes. They pulled up in front of the man's home where he was wadding in water that was just coming up to his front door. They asked him to come with them, but the man refused and said, "I'm a true believer, God will provide for me."

Hours later a major river crested over its banks and the man fled up his stairs to the second floor of his home. As he hung out the window a boat came for him and once again, he refused to go with them and said, "I'm a true believer, God will provide for me."

Day turned to night and then the local dam burst. Water was flooding so fast the man had to climb up to the roof on his house. The rain was still coming down in buckets when suddenly, a light came peering through the clouds and rain. A thunderous roar came over the man and his home. It was a helicopter and the pilot tried to pick up the man, but he refused to go, saying "I'm a true believer, God will provide for me."

Well, the waters kept coming. Soon the man was swept away and drowned all alone in the swift raging currents of the flood.

When he appeared before God in heaven, he asked God, "I don't understand. I've been a good man and devoted my entire life to honoring and believing in you. Why didn't you provide for me?" God said to him, "I sent a truck, a boat and a helicopter to save you. What didn't you understand?"

If this believer truly understood faith, he would have had the wisdom to recognize God's interventions and understood when and how He bestows His mercy and grace upon us.

Chapter 18
Spiritual Journeys Never End

It took me thirteen years to complete this book and what I thought was my spiritual journey. In retrospect, I've spent a lifetime on this journey and only after I recognized and accepted ADC signs from my father-in-law and parents, did I discover an unwavering faith.

My wife Jody and I returned to Naples Florida during the second year of the COVID-19 coronavirus pandemic. Before we left on our long drive south, my daughter Jessica gave me a book to read titled "Signs, The Secret Language of the Universe," by Laura Lynne Jackson.

When we finally arrived at the condo in Naples, I began to unpack my bags and hang all my clothes in the walk-in closet. Jody was exhausted and fell fast asleep, but I was wide awake, and I thought it would be a nice gesture to unpack and hang all of Jody's clothes.

As I was walking in and out of the closet, I kept finding coins on the floor. It was very peculiar because I'd pick them up, look around the floor for more coins but found nothing. As I repeatedly walked in and out of the closet somehow more coins would appear on the floor. This continued for three or four trips in and out of the closet before I stopped finding coins.

The following day I began to read the book Jessica gave me. The author, Laura Lynne Jackson, is a well credentialed psychic medium, a high school English teacher, wife, and mother of three. She is certified by the Windbridge Institute for Applied Research in Human Potential and the Forever Family Foundation, specializing in afterlife science, grief, and bereavement.

In her book, Jackson speaks of many different signs that can be interpreted as ADCs. She mentioned numbers, which are connections I have with my father, as well as butterflies and rainbows that I experience with my mother. She also listed finding coins as an ADC sign, but at that time I didn't think of any spiritual connection or what this sign could mean to me.

Then it hit me … my mother-in-law Grace, died in 1994 at the young age of 68. We were very close, but she died before my heart, spirit and mind were opened up and I discovered unwavering faith. As a Captain in the Newark Fire Department, my father-in-law never made more than $21,000 a year, and he always credited my mother-in-law for her financial skills and money smarts. Grace was an excellent budgeter and money manager who together with my father-in-law created assets of four homes on Long Beach Island and an impressive stock and bond portfolio. After all those years, I finally had my personal spiritual connection with my loving mother-in-law.

Jackson also wrote about a little boy who before he passed would ask his mother to take a picture of a clock when the numbers appeared as 11:11. I literally just finished reading the chapter and as I got up from the couch, I noticed the screen on our Alexa brightly displaying the numbers 11:11. I was stunned, amazed, and snapped a picture of the displayed time with my phone. By now you know, I don't believe in coincidences and the number 11:11 continued to appear at random times and it seemed like someone was trying to let me feel their presence. Finally, I said out loud, "Hey Dad, thanks for continuing to give me confirmation. I love you and miss you."

Ninth Butterfly Sighting

The following day was spectacular and the perfect weather to play a round of golf with my friends. I consider myself to be a mid-to-high handicap hacker, but still enjoy playing competitive rounds. I was on the 16th hole of the gold course at Tiburon, in Naples Florida, which is a 165-yard par three. Off the tee my ball landed just 6 – 8 feet from the cup. As I approached the green, a beautiful large black and orange Monarch butterfly flew up to me and circled around me a few times. As I lined up my putt, I acknowledged my mother and once again said out loud, "Please mom help me make this putt for birdie." I typically get the jitters standing over a putt, but for some reason I felt a complete sense of calm and reassurance as I sunk the putt to win the hole. I thanked my mother and told her I love and miss her.

As you know, I'll pray while I'm driving and after thanking God for all His blessings, I'll have a quick word with my parents, father-in-law, and mother-in-law. I was driving to play another round of golf when I realized my father, mother and mother-in-law were giving me their special personal signs, but it had been a while since I heard from my father-in-law. So, I said "Hey Pop, I haven't heard from you in some time, please give me a sign that only you and I would recognize. Something personal and unique that would prove to me you're still watching over us." I drove for about one tenth of a mile when on the side of the road a big blue and white sign with the word 'Serenity' printed on it appeared. The billboard was an incredible sign and provided me a resounding message that he is always with me and continues to give me his personal confirmation.

I had been using one of the spare bedrooms at our condo as an office, but friends were coming to visit so I had to rearrange the furniture to accommodate their stay. Suddenly, as I moved a dresser, a bright, shiny penny appeared from underneath the furniture. I looked at the date and it was 2018, the year my mother had died.

I just finished reading "Signs, The Secret Language of the Universe" when one of my best friends, Frank, called. He wanted to tell me he was watching a Netflix series called "Surviving Death" and was a little spooked out. He told me the program was about the afterlife and that a psychic medium named Laura Lynne Jackson was featured in two episodes. Frank's a skeptic and a data-driven individual, but he had to admit Jackson seemed very credible and impressive. Frank had no idea I had just finished reading her book, and since I don't believe in coincidences, a spiritual connection was once again being presented to me. I watched the series and learned one of the main intentions was to help protect innocent grieving people from psychic frauds who were out to make a quick buck.

While the program discredited fake psychic mediums, it also established legitimate scientifically credible psychic mediums, of which Laura Lynn Jackson was featured and endorsed.

What I like about Jackson is she relates ADCs as signs from God, which she defines as the universe, our spiritual guides or guardian angels and loved ones who have crossed. Together they make up our "Team of Light" that are always there to guide and support us.

Much like biblical prophets, creditable modern-day psychics can provide hope and proof of a higher power, faith in an afterlife and comfort to those with grieving broken hearts.

Recognizing and believing in the signs from loved ones who have passed can help to restore one's faith and develop a more meaningful and loving relationship with God.

Psalm 31:1-2 God is Our Refuge

In you, O Lord, I have taken refuge; Let me never be put to shame; deliver me in Your righteousness. Turn Your ear to me, come quickly to my rescue, be my rock of refuge.

I've been blessed to have had multiple unique experiences that proved to me, without any question or doubt, that there is an afterlife, and that God truly does exist.

I'm thankful to God for opening my eyes to what can't be seen, my mind to what is beyond the obvious, and my heart to those who are judged without representation or understanding. By witnessing His work through loved ones immediately after their passing, God showed me He exists. He, exhibited His righteous and ever-present love, and I was so fortunate to have Him give me the gift of unwavering faith. This gift was first presented to me in August of 2008 and subsequently has been reinforced many times thereafter.

As everyone knows, life is filled with wonderful times of celebration, but sadly it is also filled with periods of extreme stress and points of unbearable sorrow. I didn't realize it back in August of 2008, but the gift of unwavering faith was the most wonderful, and precious gift God could give to anyone.

You see, unwavering faith is the true belief that God is always there, and He is always listening. God gives me permission to call him up and have an open, truthful, two-way conversation anytime and anywhere. A two-way communication may seem unbelievable to some people, but if you've been blessed to have unwavering faith, you can hear God when He speaks. He turns His ear to me and answers my every prayer, every wish, and every request. God has never let me down.

He has rescued me during the darkest of times and is truly my rock and refuge.

My Prayer

God grant me the wisdom, the strength, the compassion, and the patience to be the best person I can possibly be. Help me to always walk in Your light and to keep Jesus Christ in my mind, my heart, and my soul.

God, thank you for the wonderful gift of unwavering faith You have bestowed upon me and guide me as Your disciple to encourage others to discover Your grace and righteousness.

Amen

There are no endings … Just new beginnings!

Appendum

Layman Devotionals

Our church produces a book of Lenten Devotionals written by members of our congregation. Reverend Jen Van Zandt chooses scriptures and members select passages they feel are close to their hearts or supports a spiritual message they'd like to share. Obviously, I enjoy reading and writing content presented in a devotional style format. It's been the cornerstone to my spiritual journey and writing devotionals has enriched my biblical knowledge. The process is a wonderful way to reassess your life and strengthen your relationship with God.

The following pages are examples of devotionals I've written, and I encourage you to try your hand at writing a devotional. I'm confident you'll find the experience enlightening and spiritually fulfilling.

Psalm 23 The Devine Shepherd

The Lord is my Shepherd, I shall not want. He makes me lie down in green pastures; He leads me beside still waters; He restores my soul. He leads me down the right paths for His name's sake. Even though I walk through the darkest valley, I shall fear no evil; for You are with me; Your rod and Your staff they comfort me. You prepare a table for me in the presence of my enemies; You anoint my head with oil; my cup overflows. Surely goodness and mercy shall follow me all the days of my life, and I shall dwell in the house of the Lord my whole life long.

Daily Relection

Being CEO to several companies I was expected to be their best salesperson and I typically sold clients products and services we didn't offer. I had total faith in my own capabilities and never doubted my ability to reinvent our companies and keep my client promises. Our companies flourished and as a naive young man, I thought it was all me.

As I matured and faced challenges that were completely out of my control, I realized having faith in myself just wasn't enough and spiritually foolish.

So, I began reciting Psalm 23 every morning. It reminds me God is always present and that I'm truly never alone. Through prayer I can feel the Holy Spirit guiding me and I seek God's influence in helping me to make decisions. Sensing the presence of Jesus Christ is especially important when my judgements will impact people's lives. Knowing I can connect with God at any time and seek His guidance is comforting and leads me to make smarter, better choices and decisions.

During the most difficult of times, God is there listening to my prayers. His answers convert monumental challenges into manageable actions, transfers doubt into hope, replaces fear with reassurance and turns stress into relief. God provided David the poetic talent to pen Psalm 23 providing each of us the security to know that even in death, God will be there to comfort us. God's hand touches everything in my life including my business activities and competitive negotiations. Once I surrendered my old ego to God, I began to truly believe He will always provide for me.

Daily Prayer

God, You have blessed me, my family and friends beyond my wildest dreams and aspirations. Thank you for placing Your mercy and grace upon my head no matter where I am, or where I go ... I am forever in Your house.

Amen

John 15:1 -2 Jesus the True Vine

"I am the true vine, and my Father is the vine grower. 2 He removes every branch in me that bears no fruit. Every branch that bears fruit He prunes to make it bear more fruit."

Daily Reflection

I helped Reverend Jen with this year's Confirmation class, and we had a wonderful experience discussing and studying John 15: 1 - 2 with the students. To provide a visual reinforcement, Reverend Jen asked the class to draw a vine leading to a vineyard filled with grapes. It was a collaborative project, and I was delighted to watch the students support each other as they created a vineyard that was flourishing and sprawling with a big vine filled with grapes. It was interesting to hear the different interpretations and see the various types of vines, and it was encouraging to see the students light up when God's message clicked in. The exercise initially took me back to visiting vineyards in Napa Valley and Tuscany, but as the class continued, I realized we were the vine doing God's work.

We were pruning the student's branches and providing spiritual guidance to a generation who could strengthen the Christian vine and hopefully keep the vineyard fruitful for future generations.

Good fruit represents a Godly life, filled with noble virtues and possessing a loyal respected character. This is a life we all should aspire to live, but it can be challenging considering the barrage of violence, discrimination, and controversial negative news we're subjected to on a daily basis.

To remove all this negative worldly energy, our branches require constant care and pruning. When I need to feel the vine grower's gracious and merciful touch I read scripture; discuss bible passages with friends; attend service; and pray. I also speak with God and ask Him for blessings at home, in the car, the office, anywhere and anytime I want to feel His presence and when I need the Holy Spirit to guide me.

Life is fruitful when we accept Jesus as the true vine and God as the vine grower.

Daily Prayer

God, please place your goodness and grace upon me and let me feel the presence of the Holy Spirit directing and guiding me to do your work. Help me to be the best possible person I can be and an inspirational mentor to all those who want and need my assistance. And God, please give me the wisdom, strength, patience, courage, compassion, and endurance to be a good disciple as I do my best to walk in the light of my Lord and Savior Jesus Christ.

Amen

John 15:12-13 No Greater Love

"This is my commandment, that you love one another as I have loved you. No one has greater love than this, to lay one's life down for one's friends."

Daily Reflection

When I read this scripture, I immediately think of our men and women in service, police, firefighters, and all our first responders. These courageous people put their lives on the line every day and they do it for complete strangers. Society often refers to them as heroes and their typical response is always, "We're not heroes, we're just doing our job." I'm confident I'd lay my life down for my wife, children, most definitely my grandchildren and probably my favorite family members and friends. But I'm not sure I could literally lay my life down like Jesus did. Besides our brave men and women in uniform, I don't really know anyone that would honestly die for a stranger. They may say they'd lay their lives down for a stranger but that's easier said than done. Christ's love was not only in words, but also in his sacrificial death for all of us, those he knew, those that knew of Him and for all of us here today and generations to come who will follow His teachings.

There is no greater love than to lay one's life down for one's friend. The key and definitive message here is love … love … love! And God's Commandment is simply to love one another as He loves each of us. But He doesn't want us just to speak of love, because words are meaningless without actions that support the words. Just as Christ didn't just speak of love, He proved His love with the ultimate act of laying His life down for all of us ... His friends. So, speak of love, but back the words up with true acts of kindness, compassion, forgiveness, patience, and personal sacrifice when a friend is in need.

So, these three things continue forever: faith, hope and love. And the greatest of these is love. 1 Corinthians 13:13

Daily Prayer

God, please grant me the ability to forgive and forget, and remove any feelings of vengeance, anger, or hostility from my heart. Grant me the wisdom to understand what isn't known and the vision to see what isn't obvious. Let the Holy Spirit guide me and let me feel Your presence so I will be capable of living of to Your greatest command of loving others, as you always love me.

Amen

Psalm 139: 23-24 Following God's Ways

Search me, O God, and know my heart.
Try me and know my anxious thoughts.
And see if there be any hurtful way in me;
And lead me in the everlasting way.

Daily Reflection

There have been many times in my life when I felt like Job. In Job 31:6, Job says, "Let God weigh me in honest scales, and He will know that I am blameless." While Job's faith was repeatedly tested, I don't really believe God is testing me. But I do believe God is examining my heart, my soul and my overall self-being. Since I truly believe God knows all, it doesn't make sense that He would test my faith, because He already knows my faith is unwavering and cannot be challenged or questioned. But having other aspects of your life examined by God is important because in today's hectic and chaotic world it's too easy for us as humans to sin and forget the teachings of Jesus Christ.

In my opinion, being perpetually examined by God is a very good and positive thing. If you believe you are watched or examined by God, you will naturally be more conscious to live by the teachings of Jesus Christ. This means doing more than what's obviously right or wrong, it means taking your life to a much higher level of compassion, love, forgiveness and caring for others.

God helps me recognize when I'm heading down an unrighteous path and keeps my feet planted, my head and heart in the right place and God helps me to be the best person I can possibly be.

Daily Prayer

God, help me to be the best possible person I can be. The best possible son, husband, father, grandfather, brother, uncle, cousin, friend, mentor to future business leaders and deacons. To do so, God lead me and guide me to always walk in the light of my Lord and Savior Jesus Christ and help me to live every day of my life by Your teachings.

Amen

Mathew 6:7-13 The Lord's Prayer

Our father who art in heaven, hallowed be thy name, thy kingdom come, on earth as it is in heaven. Give us this day Your daily bread and forgive us of our sins as we forgive those who sin against us. And lead us not into temptation, but deliver us from evil, for Thine is the kingdom, the power and glory, forever and ever, Amen.

Daily Reflection

Growing up as a Roman Catholic, repetition of prayers was the accepted or normal way to pray. After confessing your sins to a priest, you'd be given penance that consisted of repeating a couple of standard prayers …

"Say three Our Fathers and four Hail Mary's and you're good to go." And repeatedly reciting the Rosary may be a form of meditation or connection at some level, but it just never made sense to me.

I felt this type of praying contradicted how Jesus taught us to pray with the Lord's Prayer. I found that repetitive style of praying to be incredibly boring and frankly not meaningful, so I didn't pray as often as I do today.

As I spiritually matured, I learned a whole new way of praying. It's conversational, I rarely repeat myself with my newfound method of praying and I make a real connection with God, with my words finally having meaning. And now, every time I recite the Lord's Prayer, I truly feel a deeper, more meaningful purpose in God's words. The Lord's Prayer really is the Disciple's Prayer since it was meant as an example of praying for all God's disciples. I also find it very interesting that the format of The Lord's Prayer has six petitions. The first three are dedicated specially to God's holiness and explaining God as the almighty judge who will bestow his saving grace upon all of us when it's our time to enter His kingdom. In the last three petitions of prayer, we ask God to help us with our daily challenges and needs, to forgive us for what we do wrong, and remind us not to be judgmental and to forgive those that do us wrong, and to give us the strength to fight everyday temptations that will lead us down an unrighteous path.

Daily Prayer

Thank you, Jesus, for teaching me how to pray, for always being there and listening to me, for answering all my prayers, and forever connecting me to You with Your ever loving grace.

Amen

Luke 6:36-37 Do Not Judge, Be Merciful

Be merciful, just as your Father is merciful. Do not judge, and you will not be judged; do not condemn, and you will not be condemned. Forgive, and you will be forgiven.

Daily Reflection

This is part of a much broader text describing how we should treat our enemies. However, my interpretation of an enemy doesn't necessarily mean an army we are at physical war with. I believe they are also terrible acts committed by people we love who have in some horrible way hurt, betrayed, or disrespected us. They may have behaved in an offensive manner, caused pain and suffering, or committed sinful acts like stealing or lying and have shown a total disregard of other's feelings. As humans, our natural reactions are to become angry and revengeful. But during these most difficult and emotionally charged times, we need to find God's love within us – love and remember our role as Christians and disciples of Jesus Christ. We are all God's children, and He bestows His graciousness and mercy on all of us, as well as those undeserving. Being created in God's image, we must find our inner self-discipline to forgive those undeserving individuals, so we can bestow our graciousness and mercy on them.

But this is truly difficult because all throughout our lives we have learned and been conditioned to judge. We have an opinion on movies, food, cars, clothes, computers, authors, everything, and anything. We are conditioned to judge, that's how we determine right from wrong, good from bad, what we like and what we don't like. And unfortunately, we can't help ourselves from judging others. But God does not judge, and He does not condemn. God's measurement in us is not judgement, it's mercy.

Jesus taught us anyone who passes judgement is a hypocrite. And He told us to remove the log from our own eye, so we can see clearly and help our brother to remove the speck from his eye. This is probably the most difficult of all God's teachings and for a human being to successfully attain. But it's certainly something we should all strive to accomplish and aspire to achieve.

Daily Prayer

God give me the absolute love to forgive, the ultimate discipline to never judge, the abundance of wisdom to accept all people, and the compassion to bestow graciousness and mercy on everyone, especially those who have sinned against me.

Amen

1 Corinthians 13:14-16 Love is Patient

Love is patient; love is kind; love is not envious or boastful or arrogant or rude. It does not insist on its own way; it is not irritable or resentful; it does not rejoice in wrongdoing but rejoices in truth.

Daily Reflection

These are two short sentences in a series of profound letters written by Apostle Paul to the people of Corinth. These words also represent a small portion of popular scripture recited in many Christian marriage ceremonies. And while these words serve as wonderful advice to couples making a lifelong commitment to one another, they are insightful words that we as Christians should not only live by, but also aspire to feel deep inside out hearts and souls.

Sacrificing your time to feed, clothe and care for those less fortunate can be viewed as acts of love. But in my opinion, these are simply moral acts of kindness that we as Christian should be doing.

Love is much more. It's total control – an indescribable sense of peace and tranquility that comes over you during the most stressful and difficult of times. Love is feeling the Holy Spirit inside of you, providing patience, unquestionable forgiveness and understanding. Love is feeling God taking over your body, mind, and soul as He carries you through the most challenging times of your life.

God is always with us, and you'll recognize His presence when you feel this unique divine, spiritual feeling of love.

Daily Prayer

God guide me to live by the book of James. Give me the patience to be quick to listen, and the strength to be slow to speak, and when I do, put inspiring words of wisdom in my mind and my mouth. Please help me to forgive and to control my emotions so I will be slow to anger. Let mercy replace my judgement of others and comfort me with Your everlasting presence.

Amen

Romans 5:3-5 Hope Does not Disappoint

And not only that, but we also boast in our sufferings, knowing that suffering produces endurance, and endurance produces character, and character produces hope, and hope does not disappoint us, because God's love has been poured into our hearts through the Holy Spirit that has been given to us.

Daily Reflection

We plan our futures, but God always has a better plan for us. I spent years looking for a business successor to my last company, SGW and several times thought I had the perfect suitor. While it was a frustrating challenge, I never lost hope, I surrendered my destiny to God and waited patiently to have my prayers answered.

During an awards ceremony, I sat next to Beverly, a woman who worked for SGW, the company I was praying for. I typically count things in a room like lights, ceiling tiles and number of people. Turning to Beverly I asked if she noticed anything peculiar in the room of over 500 people. She looked over the crowd and said, "No, not really." So, I questioned, "Didn't you notice that beside a waiter and three college interns, you're the only other person of color in this entire ballroom?" Beverly laughed and replied, "Oh, I'm used to that." I immediately felt the Holy Spirit and I knew God was about to change my life, Beverly's life and SGW's future forever.

I knew nothing of Beverly's background, but quickly learned her extraordinary life's journey. She came from humble beginnings in

East Orange, NJ; transferred from Clifford J. Scott High School to Citadel of Hope Academy; cared for an ill mother and sister with special needs; worked to pay her own tuition; and was Valedictorian of her class; at Berkley College served as President of Phi Beta Lambda, (America's future business leaders). Before SGW, she worked at Prudential and KPMG; lost her first daughter after a complicated pregnancy; feels blessed to have given birth to a son and daughter; adopted her sister's son and more. Every challenge made her stronger and helped develop her righteous character.

Successful succession plans take years of planning and vetting, but sometimes it just takes a unique event or what I believe is God's intervention. On September 17, 2019, Beverly became President, CEO, and majority shareholder of SGW. By October 30, 2019, SGW received its Minority Women Business Enterprise (MWBE) Certification from NJ's Department of Treasury.

Daily Prayer

God thank you for giving me the ability to receive and feel the Holy Spirit and for opening my eyes, heart and mind to Your presence, direction, and guiding hand. You never disappoint...

Amen

Additional Biblical Scholar Interpretations of Numerical References

Three

The Father, the Son, and the Holy Spirit – Holy Trinity.

God is omnipresent being everywhere, omnipotent all powerful, and omniscient all knowledgeable.

God knows the past, the present, and the future.

Major Israel feast seasons (Exodus 23:14-19).

Times of daily prayer (Daniel 6; Psalms 55:17).

Sacrifice of three-year old animals (Genesis 15:9).

Three days and three nights after the resurrection of Jesus (John 2:19).

Jesus taught his disciples for three years about the same amount of time as his ministry on earth.

Four

Corners of the earth (Isaiah 11:2).

Number of dominant kingdoms (Daniel 7:3).

Number of seasons and directions on the earth.

Four types of soil (Matthew 13).

Number of pillars in the Temple.

Six

Man created on the sixth day (Genesis 1:31).

Number of days to work.

Is also imperfect and is the opposite of the Holy Trinity in 666 (Revelation 13:18). Number of cities God gave the Levites for refuge (Numbers 35:6).

Eight – Not very significant

Represents victory.

Circumcision performed on the 8th day.

Number of people on Noah's ark.

Nine – Also not a very significant number.

Number of fruits listed in Galatians 5:22-24. However, this probably isn't a complete list of all of the fruit of the Spirit.

Ten represents law and order.

Governments and laws.

The Ten Commandments (Exodus 20).

Number of Elders in the majority of city gates (Ruth 4:2).

Number of Tribes in Israel's Northern Kingdom (1 Kings 11).

Twelve

Number of governmental perfection and God's divine authority or sovereignty.

Tribes of Israel.

Twelve disciples and after the death of Judas included Apostle Paul.

Groups of twelve in Ezekiel 's description of the construction of the heavenly temple (Ezekiel 48); there were twelve foundations, twelve angels, and twelve gates in the New Jerusalem Temple. The walls of the Temple had twelve foundations and there the twelve names were written of the twelve apostles (Revelation 21:14).

Thirty associated with sorrow or fasting.

It represents affliction as Aaron was mourned for 30 days (Numbers 20:29) as was Moses (Deuteronomy 34:8), and Jesus was betrayed for 30 pieces of silver (Matthew 27:3-5).

Forty associated with trials and period of human testing.

Rained for 40 days and 40 nights (Genesis 7:4).

Number of years Israel wandered the Wilderness (Numbers 14:33).

Days and nights Moses went up into the clouds on Mount Sinai.

Number of days and nights Jesus tempted by Satan and fasted alone in the Wilderness (Matthew 4:2).

Fifty significant to the Jews.

Year of Jubilee for the forgiveness of debt by debtors (Leviticus 25:10).

Pentecost was celebrated on the 50th day after Passover (Leviticus 23:15-16). The day that the Church of Jesus Christ was founded (Acts 2).

The Holy Spirit came to everyone in the church 50 days after the resurrection of Jesus Christ's indicating the Holy Spirit is inside all who believe.

Seventy associated with human justice, judgment, and laws.

Number of Elders in Israel that helped to make judgments (Numbers 11:16).

 Prophet Ezekiel saw 70 Elders in the House of Israel (Ezekiel 8:11).

Number of years Israel was in captivity by the Babylonians (Jeremiah 29:10).

Special Dedication

Genesis 2:24

Therefore a man leaves his father and mother and clings to his wife. And they become one flesh.

I want to thank my wife Jody, my partner in life and soulmate. The foundation to every one of our successes was her unquestionable devotion and faith in my capabilities. Jody has supported me throughout my entire life, and she is my emotional stabilizer as I navigated through the constant changing ebb and flows of business.

She mended my heart when it was broken, my mind when I was confused, she kept my feet and ego planted and nursed me back to health after a multitude of weird medical conditions.

Jody gave me life's most precious gifts … two beautiful, healthy, and loving children Kristofer and Jessica, who chose amazing, loving, and devoted spouses … my daughter-in-law Sue and son-in-law Mike. Together they brought into the world six of the most wonderful, adoring, and special grandchildren … in chronological order: Nicholas (Nicky), Joseph (Joey), Sofia (Fi-Fi), Giavanna (Gi-Gi) Sienna (Si-Si) and Michael David (Mikey).

John 15:12–17 True Meaning of a Friend

"This is my commandment, that you love one another as I have loved you. No one has greater love than this, to lay down one's life for one's friends. You are my friends if you do what I command you. I do not call you servants any longer, because the servant does not know what the master is doing; but I have called you friends, because I have made known to you everything that I have heard from my Father. You did not choose me, but I chose you. And I appointed you to go and bear fruit that will last, so that the Father will give you whatever you ask Him in my name. I am giving you these commands so that you may love one another."

Jody and I are a very rich couple, but I'm not speaking in financial terms. Together, we've acquired unsurmountable riches and created an uncountable fortune of what I feel are lives most precious commodities … true friends.

God has blessed us with an extraordinary number of great friends who we can count on regardless of the time of day or night. The number of pages in this book would easily be doubled if I listed each person by name and described our relationships.

Proverbs 18:24

Some friends play at friendship, but a true friend sticks closer than one's kin.

True friends can be closer than family and we are blessed to have true friends that have provided us great strength and support during the most stressful of times.

Psalm: 119:63

I am a companion of all who fear you, of those who keep your precepts.

We inherit our family and are given no alternative, but God gives us an opportunity to choose our friends. There is an old proverb attributed to Benjamin Franklin: "lie down with dogs ...get up with fleas." John Webster also wrote in his play "The White Devil" in 1612 "For they that sleep with dogs, shall rise with fleas."

But this advice was originally given by Apostle Paul in

1 Corinthians 15:33

Do not be deceived: Bad company ruins good morals.

Proverbs 22:6

Train children how to live right, and when they are old, they will not change.

I especially wrote this book for the six special loves of my life who all call me Poppy. A special note to my grandchildren:

Proverbs 4:10-11

My child, listen and accept what I say. Then you will have a long life. I am guiding you in the way of wisdom, and I am leading you on the right path.

Most everyone wrestles with faith and believing in God. But whenever you have any doubts, read my testimonials. Believe in what I have witnessed and hopefully my words will provide the spiritual nourishment you'll need to help you through life's most difficult, stressful challenges and in the process, restore your personal faith.

Be humble, live by the golden rule and put all your worries in God's hands. Your prayers will always be answered, and God will never let you down.

And remember, I will always be with you.

Love,

Poppy

Special Acknowledgements

Proofreading and editing are extremely important vetting phases that must be completed prior to publishing and printing a book. The people I selected came from diversified backgrounds, are critically honest and able to provide constructive criticism and enlightening recommendations. While some were chosen for their ability to evaluate content, others were picked for their exceptional spelling and grammatical skill sets. Seventeen individuals participated who I respect, admire, and trust would never let me make a fool of myself.

These special people are as follows:

Jody K. Scelba – is my wife, soulmate and without question my toughest, most unbashful, critic.

Jody will be the first one to call me out if I exaggerate an event or embellish on a particular point.

Jody's proofreading was critical because she traveled the spiritual journey with me, and she witnessed my spiritual transformation first-hand.

The only thing she may challenge or question is anywhere I mention my humility. But overall, she confirmed all the events as I described them in this book to be true and factual.

Thanks Jody, for being my loving, adoring wife, for having faith in me, and for being my #1 fan for all these years.

Love you forever!

JESSICA S. CURRAN – is my loving devoted daughter and one of my staunches and toughest critics.

When it comes to feelings and emotions, Jessie takes right after me, and we both wear them on our sleeves. We can give a tough, no nonsense exterior, but we cry over sentimental heart-tugging TV commercials.

Between raising three children and working, Jess has a very hectic, crazy, and stressful schedule like so many other young mothers.

Attending church on Sundays is becoming more difficult for young parents simply because of all the conflicting activities and I'm hoping this book may help them to maintain a spiritual foundation and to keep the faith.

Jess, thanks for being you ...

I love you honey!

Kristofer D.F. Scelba – I didn't ask my son to be a proofreader because I knew it would take time from his busy work and parenting schedule.

But I'm very glad he took it upon himself to read literally every word in just one night.

I had already received final comments from everyone, and Kris provided many edits and re-write suggestions that I found to be invaluable.

While the birth of his second son Joey was a pivotal point in my spiritual Journey, it was the scariest, most stressful and faith testing point of Kris's life. He lived through some incredibly challenging times, and I'm very proud of his accomplishments.

Kris, thanks for taking a personal interest, it was a wonderful surprise.

I love you!

FRANK LABONIA – is one of my very best friends, but also one of my harshest critics.

Frank enjoys debating and over the years has been a wonderful confidant, who even when he agrees with me, will purposely play devil's advocate and without any mercy challenge me on every point.

He's 6'5" and I'm 5'6" but it doesn't matter if we're discussing historical events or playing a round of golf, we always end up becoming fierce competitors. Our competitive interactions have made me a more patient listener, holistic thinker, and basically wiser person.

Thanks Frank for helping me improve my swing, changing my putter grip and lowering my handicap.

I'm blessed to have you as my golf partner, and I look forward to many years of tee times together.

DR. BABAK HAGHIGHI – and his entire family are the most wonderful, loving, and caring people the world has ever known.

Bob is without a doubt the most interesting and knowledgeable religious layperson I have ever met.

He's a practicing Muslim but has the most biblically diversified background of anyone I know. Bob's comprehension and understanding of the Tora and the Bible's Old and New Testaments are as proficient as his knowledge of the Koran.

I love discussing all types of religious and spiritual topics and issues with him. Bob inspires me to explore scripture and dig deeper into the personal meanings of each passage.

Thanks Bob for all your love and wisdom. You're truly my brother.

Reverend Jennifer Van Zandt – is a wonderful, motivational, and inspirational minister and speaker.

In 2011, Jody and I were church shopping and one Sunday we visited The First Presbyterian Church USA of Boonton. To my delight, they had a female minister, Reverend Jen. This was the first time I watched and listened to a woman giving a sermon and to my surprise we had an instant connection.

Before Jen's calling, she was a business coach working with high-powered executives and flying around the world in private jets. Her prior business experience contributes to her unique pastoral perspective, which I truly enjoy, appreciate, and connect to.

Thanks Jen, for inviting me to contribute to our annual Lenten Devotionals. The experience served as a foundation to this book.

Hope I did you proud, God Bless.

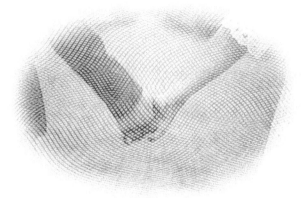

VAL AND JOHN DELLOIACONO – are two of our best and oldest friends.

While they both had traditional Protestant upbringings, they were also very open minded and respectful of other types of worship.

They found their comfort zone at the Morristown Spiritual center and since becoming members they have been active participants in the management of the church.

We have a very special something and share the same key life values that overshadow any opinion differences we may ever have. We love, accept, appreciate and are always there for each other.

Thanks Val and John, I think you'll agree, Proverbs 18:24 was written for us.

Some friends may ruin you, but a real friend will be more loyal than a brother.

MIKE AND CAROL CRITCHLEY – are a wonderful loving couple who are spiritually and emotionally connected to Jody and me.

Our families have spent many a Christmas Eve together and although we don't see each other as much as we'd like, we never feel distanced or apart.

Mike is a CPA and serves as the CFO for a large automotive retailer with multiple franchises. He also provides his professional expertise and heads his church's finance committee.

As a member of the local hospital's foundation board, Carol's prior banking experience proves to be a valuable asset in raising much-needed funds.

Mike is a Lector and Carol is an Extraordinary Minister in the Catholic Church and serves the host and wine during Mass.

Thank you Mike and Carol. No time or distance can ever separate our hearts. May God always place His mercy and blessings upon your heads.

Norm Feld – was my neighbor for over 25 years and a seasonal golf partner. He has become a dear friend and spiritual confidant.

Norm and I come from different religious backgrounds. He's Jewish and I'm a Christian, but through our many spiritual and religious conversations we've discovered our beliefs regarding God, faith and the afterlife are actually very similar.

Unfortunate events or unhappy moments can challenge anyone's faith, but the foundation of Norm's faith is simply in the extraordinary love he has for his family and friends.

Thanks Norm. You've always been a good neighbor and I sincerely appreciate your expertise, especially with the first five books.

Hope you got the joke!

Roy and Anita Mathews – are practicing Roman Catholics and attend church most every Sunday.

Roy came to America from India at age 22, and Anita arrived at age 11. Prior to retiring, Roy owned a successful seafood import company, and Anita was Director of IT for a major insurer.

Christianity represents only 2.3% of the Indian population, lagging far behind Hinduism at 79.8 % and Islam at 14.2%. Roy is a Syrian Catholic and Anita being a Syrian Orthodox is a minority within a minority. Their minority status never held them back in the business world and both are very accomplished in their fields. They accept people of all faiths, beliefs, or spirituality and proactively preach tolerance.

Thank you, Roy, and Anita. You've given me wonderful feedback and a diversified perspective. Love you guys.

Leonel Montes de Oca – is a creative genius who I affectionately, and with love, refer to as my Cuban Creative Collaborator.

Leo has the uncanny ability to read my mind, and he can literally take my unreadable scribbled notes on a paper napkin and turn them into magical visual artistic masterpieces. Leo's visuals bring my words to life and his graphic interpretations consistently go well beyond my wildest expectations.

It's said music touches the soul. Well, Leo and I are also musicians, and besides having rhythm, we can harmonize better than most creative duos.

Whatever it is, I truly enjoy the creative connection, and I thank Leo from the bottom of my heart for adding an extra special dimension to this book with his brilliant cover design, illustrations, page layouts and for partnering with me on our video podcast series.

Thanks Leo! Wishing many very happy creative collaborative years together.

PATRICK BRIGHTMAN – is the very first public relations employee I hired in 1988 when I was 33 years old, and Patrick was a young local newspaper reporter of only 23 years of age.

Patrick is not only an excellent media specialist, but also the consummate PR professional. But what makes him extra special is his integrity, moral character, and the fact I can trust him with anything.

Patrick is one of the most honorable people I know, and we not only share the same November 7th birthday, we also share the same unselfish and motivational philosophies and beliefs for managing and working with employees and clients.

Patrick lives by the "Golden Rule" and treats everyone the way he'd like to be treated.

Thanks Patrick. Looking forward to many more happy, healthy birthday celebrations.

NANCY SERGEANT – is an experienced marketing professional who truly practices what she preaches.

Nancy believes deeply in proactive professional and personal development and never stops learning. From cutting edge digital marketing strategies and initiatives to the latest meditation methods or yoga positions, Nancy is dedicated and passionate about sharing her newly found knowledge and skills with others.

This desire to inspire and help others is a valuable asset to help evaluate the spiritual relevance of the content in this book.

And what are the odds ... Nancy's husband Joe also shares a November 7th birthday?

Thanks Nancy. Please don't stop trying to make me smarter and healthier.

MEGAN REDZIA - is a brilliant and exceptionally talented media, public relations, and communications professional. Megan is one of those special blessed gifts I received from God, and thankfully I had the wisdom to recognize why He brought her into my life.

I wrote about Megan becoming a partner to Patrick Brightman in 3E Public Relations to execute my succession plan in the company I was most emotionally attached to. Together with Patrick, Megan has led their team to become one of New Jersey's most respected and successful public relations firms.

When I was actively involved in the business, Megan proofread everything I wrote: speeches; blogs; articles; brochures; scripts … literally everything. I trust Megan and wouldn't publish any work without her review and final approval.

And what are the chances to learn I attended high school with her parents and graduated in the same class as her father.

Megan, thank you for looking out for my best interests and always exceeding my highest expectations. You're truly the best!

Books and Reference Materials

During my spiritual journey, I read many different bibles and resource books to educate myself and enrich my spiritual understanding. The following is a list of some of the books I read and frequently referenced when I experienced ADCs with my father-in-law, my father, and my mother. They were also especially wonderful resources when I felt God's Devine Interventions guiding me through my most difficult challenges.

Bibles:

NRSV – NEW REVISED STANDARD VERSION

NIV – NEW INTERNATIONAL VERSION (STUDY BIBLE)

NEW AMERICAN BIBLE

NEW CENTURY VERSION

CENTENNIAL BIBLE NEW TESTAMENT

NKJV – NEW KING JAMES VERSION

THE MESSAGE OF THE QURAN

WHERE TO FIND IT IN THE BIBLE
Ken Anderson

GOD'S PROMISES FOR EVERY DAY
New Century Version Scripture

THE COMPLETE GUIDE TO THE BIBLE
Steven M. Miller

NEW TESTAMENT
Contemporary English Version

THE NEW TESTAMENT
Centennial Bible

THE BIBLE –WHY IT MATTERS TODAY
Time Inc. Books

BIBLE PROPHECY HANDBOOK

Carol Smith

UNDERSTANDING YOUR BIBLE

John A. Beck

WHAT'S SO GREAT ABOUT CHRISTIANITY

Dinesh D'Souza

THE POWER OF MYTH

Joseph Campbell with Bill Moyers

LIFE LESSONS

Elisabeth Kubler – Ross & David Kessler

THE FOUR AGREEMENTS

Don Miguel Ruiz

DOORS TO OTHER WORLDS

Raymond Buckland

WHERE IS GOD WHEN IT HURTS?

Philip Yancey

GOD NEVER BLINKS

Regina Brett

BE THE MIRACLE

Regina Brett

CAN WE SPEAK TO GOD?

Ernest Holmes

THE SECRET
Rhonda Byrne

JOURNEY OF SOULS
Michael Newton, PH.D.

A NEW EARTH, AWAKENING TO YOUR LIFE'S PURPOSE
Eckhart Tolle

THE POWER OF NOW
Eckhart Tolle

MIRACLES HAPPEN
Brian L. Weiss, M.D.

101 ANSWERS – END TIMES
Mark Hitchcock

EVIDENCE OF THE AFTERLIFE
Jeffery Long, MD with Paul Perry

THE RAGAMUFFIN GOSPEL
Brennan Manning

THE UNTETHERED SOUL
Michel A. Singer

JOURNEY OF AWAKENING
Ram Dass

THE FIVE PEOPLE YOU MEET IN HEAVEN
Mitch Albom

BLESSED IN THE DARKNESS
Joel Osteen

MANY LIVES, MANY MASTERS
Brain Weiss, M.D.

MY TIME IN HEAVEN
Richard Sigmund

THE JOY OF MEDITATION
Jack & Cornelia Addington

EVERYDAY KARMA
Carmen Harra

THE HARBINGER
Jonathan Cahn

THE HARBINGER COMPANION
Jonathan Cahn

THE PARADIGM
Jonathan Cahn

JESUS TODAY
Sarah Young

JESUS ALWAYS
Sarah Young

365 DEVOTIONS FOR HOPE
Karen Whiting

Book, Chapter, and Paragraph
Wayne I. Newland

Don't Sweat the Small Stuff …With your family
Richard Carlson, PH.D.

Jesus His Life After Death
Newsweek 2015 Easter Edition

What in The World is Going On?
Dr. David Jeremiah

Padre Pio
Kathleen Stauffer

Nostradamus … Complete Prophecies
Mario Reading

Nostradamus
Knut Boeser

Texts for Preaching Years A, B and C
Walter Brueggemann, Charles B. Cousar, Beverly R. Gaventa and James D. Newsome

The Way
Josemaria Escriva

Upper Room Daily Devotional Guide
Upper Room Books

Signs, The Secret Language of the Universe
Laura Lynne Jackson

Use the following pages to begin documenting your own Spiritual Journey.

*I hope you enjoyed reading about my spiritual journey,
and I pray you have a wonderful journey of your own.*

God Bless!

CPSIA information can be obtained
at www.ICGtesting.com
Printed in the USA
JSHW052020300423
41024JS00003B/6/J

9 781662 930416